D1033837

Basic
Alice

Edite
Marth

Desig
Craig

Photography by
William Aplin
Michael Landis

Illustrated by
Leavitt Dudley

The world of
CACTUS &
SUCCULENTS
and other water-thrifty plants

Contents

What is a succulent?

A succulent is a cactus or any other plant that stores water in its stems or leaves. In the course of developing such special talents, these plants have evolved a special kind of gardening — one filled with unique and wonderful shapes, colors, and textures.

Every gardener dreams of the ideal plant — one that has interesting structure and beautiful flowers, thrives on neglect, draws gasps of admiration from the neighbors, and comes in enough varieties to fascinate you for a lifetime. What they are dreaming of is, in a word, a succulent.

Determined adaptors

Succulents are like self-made people — successful in spite of adversity. These stubborn individualists of the plant world adapted over millions of years to great climatic changes, a feat which has resulted in unique and curious methods of survival.

Many stored water in their stems or leaves while others abandoned the land and took to the trees as epiphytes, using their roots for gripping instead of taking nourishment.

Some developed disproportionately thick rootstocks in which to store moisture and nourishment against periods of drought and searing sun. Others adapted to rocky, frigid environments.

If the secret of a succulent's success could be summed up in a single word, that word would be 'water-thrifty.' Succulents have mastered the art of water conservation. By reducing their leaf surface in order to cut down on water loss from transpiration (the plant equivalent of perspiration), and by storing water in their stems or leaves, succulents can control both the amount of water they need and the

◁

Fat, juicy leaves emanating a luminous red glow, velvety hairs rich in texture — Echeveria pulvinata is a visual definition of the word succulent.

amount they use. That, in fact, is the definition of succulent: a plant that stores water in its stems or leaves or both.

There are other water-thrifty plants besides succulents — jatrophas and dioscoreas are valued by many succulent collectors for their unique forms and interesting growth habits. They have adapted to a limited water supply by establishing a pattern of

a brief growing season and a long, leafless dormancy.

Watering requirements

Most succulents will tolerate practically anything except foot traffic. But it is important not to overwater them. Their less-than-normal moisture requirements are easy to understand when you realize that the most basic

Mamillaria 'Pink Nymph' form a pattern of repeating mounds in their nursery flat; springtime blooms add additional beauty.

A bed of Echinocactus grusonii *(golden barrel cacti), illuminated by the early morning light, has an "other worldly" look.*

characteristic of succulents is this: their unusual forms are all adaptations to very little water.

But keep in mind that it's a fallacy that succulents don't need water at all; all plants need water. Succulents grown in containers require more frequent watering than those grown in the ground. Depending upon the pots you are using — large or small, clay or plastic, light-colored or dark — the water requirements of your container-grown succulents will vary. In cool or cloudy weather, they don't get thirsty. The less sun and heat, the less evaporation there will be from both pot and plant. Careful observation and experience will help you in determining your plants' needs.

From the ones you are already familiar with — even if only hen-and-chickens, jade plant, or ice plant come to mind — you probably already know that most succulents are structurally dramatic, have interesting growth habits, require little care, and are almost pest-free. The photos in this book will give you a sampling of the vast and intriguing variety of size, shape, texture, and color that awaits your discovery.

A family matter

What is the difference between succulent and cactus? It's really quite simple: succulent is the descriptive term for all plants that store water in their leaves or stems; cactus is the name of a large family of plants, all of which are succulent. The rule is this: all cacti are succulents, but not all succulents are cacti.

It is not true, though sometimes said, that spines are the distinguishing characteristic between cacti and succulents. There are cacti that are not prickly, and prickly succulents that are not cacti. Cacti have areoles (spine cushions) and two other succulents, even if they are spiny, lack these spine cushions. Plants are classified into botanical families on the basis of their reproductive systems — not by external characteristics such as leaf form or flower color or habitat or even degree of prickliness.

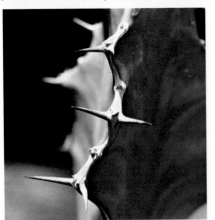

The spine cushion (areole) that distinguishes cacti and other succulents is easy to see when comparing this Euphorbia pseudocactus *(top) and* Ritterocereus pruinosis *(bottom).*

Something for every gardener

The apartment gardener who has only a sunny windowsill, the commuter who needs patient plants, the collector looking for the unusual, the arts-and-crafts enthusiast who incorporates plants into his artwork — all will find succulents absorbing and satisfying plants. The variation in color, form, size, and drought-resistance among the thousands of succulents is surprising to the uninitiated. It is entirely possible to get hooked on succulents without ever tangling with a prickly one. This richness of variety accounts for the wide appeal of succulents.

Do you want a single stunning piece of living sculpture for your office? Try an elkhorn euphorbia *(Euphorbia lactea 'cristata')*. Do you want an exquisite pale green rosette that doesn't require spraying and pruning? Try aeoniums. How about growing Boston beans *(Sedum stahlii)* in the front yard? If you have a flair for the exotic you may want Hottentot fig *(Carpobrotus)*. Maybe you'd like to go in for manufacturing tequila in a small way — plant some blue agave *(Agave tequilana)* and wait patiently — about 25 years.

If you're an armchair traveler, a collection of orchid cacti will inspire many an imaginary jungle expedition.

As for impressing the neighbors, an orchid cactus in bloom with its fragrant six-inch wide flowers will probably give you a reputation for horticultural genius. So will a night-blooming cactus. Have a party and invite friends over to watch your *Hylocereus undatus* unfold its cream-white blossoms as it perfumes the night air.

If an African safari is beyond your budget, how about a collection of the curiously bulbous plants of South Africa's arid lands with names like elephant's-foot *(Dioscorea elephantipes)*? Perhaps you're a busy city dweller with a small apartment who has little time and less space — succulents are remarkably undemanding and many of them are content to remain in the same pot for years.

Succulents come in a vast variety of sizes from a 25-foot saguaro cactus to tiny living rocks (lithops), scarcely distinguishable from pebbles. The shapes vary from formal, fluted columns to plump, little baby toes; from long-haired cylinders to sculptured

This long, slender Cephalocereus palmeri *has both sharp, stiff spines and soft, hairy spines, which develop as the plant matures.*

rosettes. There are many that you already know and many more that you'll enjoy meeting — old-man cactus (*Cephalocereus senilis*), painted-lady (*Echeveria derenbergii*), bishop's-cap (*Astrophytum myriostigma*), and drunkard's dream (*Hatiora salicornioides*).

Whether you want the extraordinary or the ordinary, the strange or the beautiful, there's a collection of succulents for indoors or out that will intrigue you for years.

Speaking Botanese

Don't be dismayed by botanical names. Wherever a common name exists for a plant, we have listed it with a plant's botanical name. However, some plants have several common names and others have none. Botanical nomenclature has a definite advantage — every known plant has a name and that same name is used by horticulturists and botanists throughout the world.

Many people panic at the mere sight of an unpronounceable botanical name. To help you overcome that problem we've spelled words phonetically in the gallery chapter, on page 47. You'll find that names become less strange as you learn that they are descriptive. To illustrate, we've translated a couple of the names from Botanese into basic English. You can see how these apparently mysterious words actually make sense.

Aeonium growing in an old stone wall: a perfect example of Nature's symmetry.

Astrophytum myriostigma (bishop's-cap).

For those who think all cacti are full of spines and geometric in shape, Rhipsalis capilliformis *will come as a surprise — it's a cactus!*

Latin spoken here

Latin or sometimes Greek is used for scientific names because it is a dead language and therefore not in a constant state of change, as spoken languages are. The botanical name is usually composed of two Latin or Greek words: one indicates the general group or genus; and the other describes the species, or specific plant.

For example,
Astrophytum myriostigma,
(bishop's-cap):
Astro = star
phytum = plant
myrio = many
stigma = stigma, marking.
Therefore, a *star*-shaped *plant* with *many stigmas.*

Epiphyllum oxypetalum, ('Queen of the Night' orchid cactus):
Epi = on
phyllum = leaf
oxy = pointed
petalum = petals
Therefore, a cactus that roots *on* trees, with modified branches that look like *leaves*, and flowers with *pointed petals.*

Speaking Botanese won't make your plants grow any differently, but it certainly makes talking and learning about them easier.

Cacti produce spectacular displays of color equal to flowering annuals.

Plants with a purpose— Indoors/Outdoors

Here are just a few of the many ways succulents can be used to accent your environment — as a permanent part of your landscape, in portable containers indoors or out, and in the greenhouse.

Because succulents are such determined adapters to nature's variations in climate and environment, they can be put to use in a number of ways — in the landscape, as outdoor containerized portables, or as house plants. Succulents and cacti grow equally well inside a greenhouse, providing countless hours of pleasure for the collector and plant hobbiest.

Spectacular low-maintenance landscaping is easy, provided you have well-drained soil and a mild, frost-free climate like that of Southern California or Arizona. As a basic rule, succulents in the landscape cannot tolerate heavy frosts or a hard freeze. For exceptions, see the heading "Winter-hardy succulent landscaping" on page 12.

Versatile performers

Versatility is the key word when describing succulents in the landscape. Equally at home as a doorway accent, a garden border, or on a steep hillside expanse, succulents serve as a distinctive low-maintenance alternative in your landscape.

Use your imagination when utilizing this creative group of plants in your landscape plan. A single giant saguaro *(Carnegiea gigantea)* or *Agave americana* can provide a dramatic, sculptural focal point. Or, an expanse of brightly colored sedum performs ably as a ground cover, while adding a mass of color equal to a bed of annuals. On the following pages the photos will demonstrate just a few of the varied and creative ways succu-

◁
A spectacular succulent landscape near Palm Springs, California.

lents can be used to change and beautify your home's environment.

Succulents as alternatives

Low maintenance and even lower water consumption are two of the more practical reasons for switching from thirsty lawns and time-demanding annuals to succulents. Did you know areas landscaped with succulents require only 20% of the water needed by equal-sized lawns? And succulents don't need mowing.

Just because succulents are easy to grow and consume little water doesn't mean you have to sacrifice beauty. If you want flowers, try *Kalanchoe blossfeldiana,* with its long-lived clusters of red, orange, yellow, and salmon flowers. It's hard to improve upon the elegance of an aeonium's perfect green rosette. Some of the larger succulents, such as agave or dudleya, or a large cereus cactus, can become a striking landscape element.

A collage of color, texture, and compact growth habits surrounding this walkway display the advantages of a succulent landscape.

Even the small crevices of a cut stone wall provide enough support and sustenance to keep these echeverias, crassula, and sempervivum thriving.

Different varieties of sedums and echeverias make an attractive border.

Planning the landscape design

Succulents can be used for all or parts of your garden. It's best to approach the designing of your home landscape in an organized manner. Careful planning and thinking in the early stages can eliminate wasted time, energy, and money.

Spend some time observing succulents growing in your neighborhood or visit a botanic garden that has a succulent garden to get an idea of the types of plants you like best. Consider your site. What is it now, and what do you think it can be? Note the existing structures and trees, and the climate and light exposure. At the same time, try to decide which shapes, colors, and textures you feel would complement your landscape. In general, strive for harmony, with just enough contrast to keep the overall scheme interesting.

Rock gardens

Perhaps you want to experiment with small groupings of succulents within your overall landscape. If this is the case, consider putting in a rock garden. The garden's natural textures are a perfect complement to the shapes, colors, and textures of succulents. A rock garden becomes a focal point in the landscape, providing a pleasing contrast to an expanse of green lawn. Try some *Sedum spathulifolium* and *Echeveria elegans* for low-growing plants, perhaps some *Aeonium arboreum* to add further contrast in height and color. Other succulents recommended for rock gardens are listed on page 22.

If a cut-stone wall is beginning to show its age, or if it's too new to have any charm, planting echeverias or sempervivum in the crevices will add another dimension. The same stubborn determination that inspired the succulent's evolution will keep it literally hanging on for dear life, thriving under seemingly impossible conditions.

Defining areas

Succulents are excellent plants for defining different areas of your garden. Their distinctive shapes and compact growth habits make it possible to have a neat, well-defined border surrounding flower beds, edging a walkway, or acting as a clean, linear design element that unifies landscape. When they are used as a border for water-demanding plants or a lawn, be sure that your succulents are protected from overwatering by planting them on mounds or in very fast-draining soil.

Ground covers

One of the most widespread and varied uses of succulents is as a ground cover. If you've been wondering what to plant between some stepping stones, try *Sedum acre* (gold moss sedum), or *Sempervivum tectorum*. Both are very cold-tolerant and their compact habits make them perfect in small, confined spaces. Keep in mind that succulent ground covers will not stand up to foot traffic and that most require full sun.

Sedum and several varieties of ice plant serve as excellent succulent ground covers for large expanses of flat or gently rolling landscape. *Lampranthus spectabilis* (trailing ice plant), *L. filicaulis* (Redondo creeper), *Sedum lineare* and *Sedum album* are among the most effective in providing quick, even, attractive cover.

Steep slopes are equally well treated with succulents. *Drosanthemum floribunda,* a fast, easy grower, has spectacular pink blooms and will cling to the steepest slope or drape beautifully down walls. Succulent ground covers have yet another advantage when used on steep slopes — they help to prevent erosion.

Planting ground covers

Succulent ground covers are easy to plant. Because they root so quickly and develop rapidly, it is possible to have nearly full cover within a year's growing season in a warm climate. Because succulent ground covers tend to be a bit more expensive than many others, you might find it more economical to place starter plants 16″ apart, rather than the commonly recommended 12″ centers. Once the plants are established (approximately one month after being set out) cuttings can be made and placed between the original plants. This will give fast, even, economical cover.

In the beginning, there may be a problem with weeds. If so, you have the option of pulling them or using a chemical weed killer. Once the cover is complete, weed problems should be minimal. Ice plant is especially good at strangling any weeds that stray into its path.

Easy-care gardening

Your succulent landscape, including rock gardens, ground covers and borders, requires relatively little care, especially if you make some special preparations. Most experts we spoke with said that succulents will grow in almost any soil, except those high in clay or adobe. Still, these same gardeners stressed the importance of good drainage for the most successful succulent culture.

Drainage can be improved in a number of ways. If you already have good soil, using mounds or slopes for your succulent beds will improve drainage. It is also possible to work in coarse builder's sand, sponge rock, or pumice to accelerate drainage.

Cacti (except for tropical epiphyllums and schlumbergera) generally need more drainage than other succulents. Be generous with the sand or small, coarse gravel when preparing for cacti. At the same time, keep in mind that cacti do not grow in sand alone. Like other plants, they need the nutrients supplied by organic matter in the soil.

If it seems likely that your succulents will receive more water than they need, perhaps because they border a lawn, be sure to add extra drainage material, and control the amount of water near the succulents by using mounds or slopes to direct the water toward the thirsty plants, and away from the succulents.

Your cacti and other succulents will require more water during their active spring and summer growing seasons than in winter when dormancy sets in. Water requirements will depend upon sun exposure and temperatures. Experience and careful observation should be your guide. The natural dormancy that occurs during winter, with the drop in temperature and shortening of days, reduces your plants' water requirements drastically. Give them just enough to keep them from shriveling.

The same seasonal variance holds true for fertilization requirements. Your succulents should be given light, regular feedings during their active growing season, no fertilization during winter dormancy.

Sun-loving succulents that are grown in partial shade may need some periodic trimming to maintain compactness of growth. Plants that have received a bit too much water and fertilizer may show similar lanky growth habits. When this happens, just clip off the young growth and set

Spreading pink Lampranthus spectabilis *adds a striking splash of color to hillside.*

Sedum rubrotinctum *can cover large expanses, has attractive yellow flowers.*

Entrance of oceanside home is brightened by blooming aloes and Kalanchoe blossfeldiana.

A variety of succulents, rocks, and shells combine naturally on a hillside rock garden leading down to terraced patio overlooking the beach. See photo top of page 13.

it in the ground. Succulents root quickly and easily, renewing the older plants in the landscape.

Where you are using succulents as a border, it may be necessary to trim growth to keep a clean line. The trimmings from any of your succulents can be used for many things — expanding your succulent landscape, starting indoor plants, growing succulents in a container, giving them away to make some new friends.

A totally succulent garden

The photos on this page (and upper right opposite) show several uses of succulents in one landscape. Located adjacent to the Pacific Ocean in Carlsbad, California, its owners have taken full advantage of the mild climate and the availability of diverse succulent plant material in designing this unique landscape. The front yard is a spectacular mass of bloom and color. In the back, a hillside leading down to the beach has been transformed into a huge, easy-to-care-for rock garden. Succulents are also used in containers as a means of integrating the living areas with the surrounding landscape.

Winter-hardy succulent landscaping

Even if you live in a cold-winter climate, it is possible to grow cacti and other succulents outdoors all year-round. A surprising number of succulent plants are native to cold regions, including the Rocky Mountains, Peruvian Andes and Swiss Alps. Although this group of plants does not include most of the varieties one first thinks of as cacti and succulents, these winter-hardy plants still have unique forms, structures, and an ability to adapt to nature's elements.

Three groups of plants most resistant to cold are opuntia, sedum, and sempervivum. With proper care, the species listed on page 22 will withstand the cold weather in any part of the United States.

We took our tips on how to grow winter-hardy succulents from Mr. Ben Haines, a grower who specializes in cacti and succulents tolerant of cold weather. He recommends that cultural practices be modified to suit the geographic location, amount of rain or snowfall, and minimum temperatures. As a general rule, he plants his super-hardy succulents in a very fast-draining soil that includes 9 parts of gravel and sand mixed together to one part of soil and peat, mixed.

Wherever moisture and humidity stay relatively low, as in Kansas, Mr. Haines simply plants his succulents on mounds of this soil mix and leaves them exposed to the wind and weather. The mounds help to accelerate the drainage while exposure to the wind reduces the moisture content of the surrounding soil.

In areas where precipitation is heavy and winter temperatures quite low, as in most of the northeast, Mr. Haines recommends use of a cold frame and the fast-draining soil mix. The cold frame keeps rain and snow off the succulents.

We found a cold frame in New Jersey being used to protect a bed of tender agave from the winter cold and snow. The frame collapses easily in the summer to expose a bed of exotic plants.

With some preparation and determination, many succulents can be grown in an inhospitable climate, but chances of success are improved by using only those that are really suitable for cold-winter areas. Keep in mind that succulents planted outside will have long periods of dormancy, and, consequently, slow development.

Succulents grown outdoors during the cold winter months, whether protected or not, should not be watered. Frozen water around their root systems can be disastrous. Their natural dormancy in cold weather will eliminate the need for water.

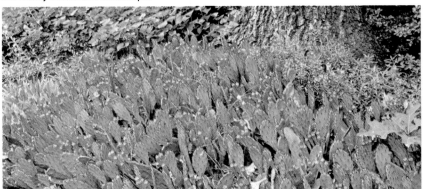

Succulents in containers grace this seaside patio, remaining consistent with the rest of the totally succulent landscape.

This healthy bed of Opuntia compressa *is growing in New York. It receives no winter protection except for the shelter provided by a large tree overhead.*

Succulents needn't grow outdoors only in California. Several varieties of sempervivum thrive without winter protection in New England.

The fiberglass cold frame outside this greenhouse shelters a bed of agave and sansevierias from winter snow and ice.

Enclosed succulent landscape offers a spectacular view from the living room.

A different kind of greenhouse

A succulent landscape, regardless of where it is located, can be enjoyed year-round if it has been completely enclosed. The photos on this page show just that. We found this oasis of sunshine, warmth and lush growth in midwinter cold on Long Island, N.Y.

This greenhouse was designed when the owner, Mrs. Louise Lippold, ran out of available windowsill space for her expanding succulent collection. Faced with a decision of reducing her collection (unthinkable) or expanding her growing space, Mrs.

Lippold came up with the perfect combination of natural landscape and specialized greenhouse.

She glassed in a south-facing patio and side yard that was visible from the living room, dining room, and kitchen. Transformed into a breathtaking landscape, the area has become the focal point of the house.

Her succulent collection is planted directly in the ground, and covered with a top dressing of pea gravel. The sculptured mounds serve to accentuate the feeling of a natural landscape, with plants grouped according to their native origins — Baja California, Mexico, South Africa, South America.

Naturalized landscape includes a collection from the southwest desert and South Africa. Plants are grouped according to native origins.

Caring for this succulent collection is a relatively simple task. The soil was prepared to be rich and porous and watering is done with a garden hose. The ideal growth conditions these plants experience have caused them to develop quite rapidly. No longer confined to pots or restricted in their access to nutrients and water, they have really "taken off" — in several instances, to Mrs. Lippold's surprise, even outgrowing the space originally allotted.

The succulent greenhouse

A more traditional answer to the problem of growing cacti and succulents in unfriendly climates can be found in the standard greenhouse. Nowadays, that standard greenhouse comes in a wide variety of sizes and shapes.

For the small-scale growers, there are window-extension units. These are available in plastic or glass versions. Larger greenhouses could be old-fashioned, sun-heated pit greenhouses (great for energy conservation), prefab units of glass or fiberglass, or even a futuristic geodesic dome model. The price range is almost as varied as the designs, providing something for all budgets, from low to high.

If you are considering a greenhouse, be sure to plan its placement carefully. Put it near your house so you can get to it easily. Greenhouses are best oriented toward the south — if you can manage it — to receive maximum benefit from the sun's warming rays. East is second best, then west; avoid the north.

Evaluate the amount of space you'll need — how big is your present collection and how much do you expect it will grow in the coming years? Realistically consider how many plants you will be able to care for, keeping in mind the amount of free time you plan on spending for gardening upkeep. A word of warning — nearly all the greenhouse growers we know agree on two points.

A greenhouse fills up *very* quickly and it is much easier and more fun to work inside an uncrowded greenhouse. Be sure to allow enough room for all your activities: repotting, propagating, growing large specimens, and storing soils, chemicals, and pots.

If you are planning on including water-demanding plants in your greenhouse, be sure to allow enough room to effectively separate your dry-growing succulents and cacti from tropical plants — they need different climates.

The variety and abundance of plant life in this enclosed landscape gives a feeling of being outdoors.

Some expert advice

Many good tips on greenhouse planning and management can be taken from the experiences of Harold and Miriam Ritzfield, active members in the New Jersey Cactus and Succulent Society. They began their greenhouse by installing a 10'x20' house that was originally a passageway in a conservatory. As their collection steadily expanded over the years, it became necessary to expand the greenhouse. They more than doubled its size by adding another 10'x20' house, with a potting and storage area between the two greenhouse sections. The original area is now used for cacti, while the addition exclusively houses other succulents.

As might be expected, their collection has kept right on growing and, at last count, was estimated to be somewhere between 3,000 and 4,000 plants, mostly in 4" pots. The Ritzfields try to keep their plants small by confining them to little pots. As collectors, it is their desire to have as many different varieties as possible within the limited space available.

They take maximum advantage of the portability of their containerized collection. As soon as warm weather arrives in the spring, the Ritzfields carry many of their plants out into the surrounding yard. This helps to reduce crowding in the greenhouse and the time that must be spent on caring for the plants. The Ritzfields have found that spring and summer rains almost eliminate the need for extra watering.

Controlling your greenhouse climate

The need for climate controls will depend upon your geographic location, the type of greenhouse you have chosen and the plants you are going to cultivate. If heating in the winter proves to be financially impractical, consider a pit greenhouse or grow plants that will tolerate low temperatures. Check the minimum temperature tolerances of specific plants in the cultural charts, page 94.

During the coldest months of the winter, most greenhouses will require some heating but, again, use the minimum temperature tolerances of your plants as a guide. A greenhouse doesn't have to be a hothouse. Plants benefit from day-to-night changes of temperature. And most plants will not suffer unduly if the temperaure drops a few degrees below their normal tolerance for a short time. Growth may slow down, but that's no catastrophe. The Ritzfields have experimented with various temperatures and found that a minimum of 55°F is best for their

When plants are grown under ideal conditions, they can develop into full-size landscape specimens, as those above.

collection. They estimate that greenhouse heating bills average around $75 per month when winters are very cold, but are quick to point out that their collection is a very important part of their lives.

The best way to evaluate the temperature of your greenhouse is to invest in a minimum-maximum thermometer. It registers the highest and lowest temperatures reached in a twenty-four-hour period. If you know what the highest and lowest temperatures have been, you can make any necessary corrections for heating or cooling.

Good air circulation is one of the most important considerations in your climate-control planning. It is vital to the health of greenhouse plants. Damp, stagnant air is an open invitation to fungus and insect infestation. A fan will supply necessary air circulation, and is well worth the investment.

Given the nearly ideal conditions of a thoughtfully designed and well-maintained greenhouse, your succulent collection will flourish. Your plants will concentrate upon growth, coloration, and flowering, instead of survival. You'll also find propagation in a greenhouse much easier, both from cuttings and from seed. For more information on propagation, see page 90.

Southern California greenhouse supplies a place to organize and propagate a collection, in addition to providing shelter from the sun and an occasional frost.

Inside the Ritzfield's greenhouse plants are grown in every available space.

A kitchen window greenhouse is the perfect place to house a small succulent collection. It also improves the view while doing daily chores.

Succulents in containers

Planting your succulents in containers, whether in clay pots or hanging baskets, will maximize the portability and flexibility of your collection. You can have succulents wherever there is room for potted plants; inside your home, on a patio, in an atrium, near an entrance-way, or hanging from an eave or tree branch. Blooming plants can be brought indoors to share their beauty. A steady rotation from outdoors to in is possible during the spring and summer, making it possible to have an ever-changing display of plants.

If you live in a cold-winter climate but stiill want the dramatic look of a side garden with *Echinocactus grusonii* (golden barrel cactus), or a beautiful bed of echeverias by the front door, containerized succulents are your answer.

Non-hardy succulents in containers can winter indoors or in your greenhouse. When the danger of frost is past, simply take the potted collection outdoors and sink the pots into the ground. Add a top dressing of pea gravel, and exotic cacti and succulents suddenly become a part of your landscape.

As with all other succulent culture, good drainage is essential. Be sure to dig a hole that's deep and wide enough to surround the pot with plenty of fast-draining soil.

Cacti look especially good in free-standing clay pottery. Their distinctive shapes and textures make them living pieces of movable sculpture, ready to complement your landscape, or your living room.

Miniature landscapes can be made with shallow dish gardens, or individual specimens in small pots can be grouped together. The possibilities for combining succulents and containers is nearly endless. A whole collection of ideas can be found in the following chapter, "Playful plants."

Hanging succulent containers

Many succulents are well suited to hanging baskets. *Sedum morganianum* (donkey's-tail), *Senecio rowleyanus* (string-of-beads), and *Ceropegia woodii* (rosary vine) all make wonderful hanging plants with their long, trailing growth. Hung on a patio or in a doorway, they are safe outside until frost. They winter inside beautifully as house plants.

Epiphyllums (orchid cacti) make spectacular hanging-basket plants. Their long, spineless branches bear

This collection of containerized cacti and other succulents can be enjoyed outdoors during warm weather, moved inside for protection when frost threatens.

Rooftop garden is landscaped exclusively with container-grown succulents. Boxes, pots, and hand-made ceramics can be moved and rearranged at owner's whim.

large, showy blooms in a wide range of colors, including white, pink, and scarlet. Because they are jungle (not desert) cacti, they require filtered shade and a soil that is rich in humus. They do well under a tree (an appropriate place for an epiphyte) or a lath overhead.

Schlumbergera cacti (formerly known as zygocactus), including the Christmas cactus (Schlumbergera bridgesii), are similar to epiphyllums in their long, spineless leaves. They too make excellent hanging-basket subjects, with an attractive display of colorful blooms.

Many other succulents can be planted in hanging containers. Varieties of rhipsalis, sedum, and echeverias, among others, are particularly well suited to hanging displays.

Keep them small

If you have limited space, container-grown succulents offer more than the convenience of portability. By keeping your collection in containers, it is possible to control the size of your plants.

If you have a giant saguaro cactus (Carnegiea gigantea) and you want to keep it under ceiling height so it will still fit in your greenhouse or living room, pot it. If you have a handsome Agave americana 'marginata,' which will bloom and die when it reaches maturity, and you'd like to postpone its demise, pot it.

Although these plants will become rootbound from remaining in a small pot, this doesn't present any serious problems. Just be sure to give them adequate water and light, frequent feedings to maintain health.

Container culture

Container culture with succulents is easy. Your plants will need a fast-draining soil that is still rich in nutrients. Because the plants are limited in their access to food and moisture, they require more water and light and more frequent applications of fertilizer during spring and summer than do succulents planted in the ground. For the needs of specific plants, consult the charts on pages 94, 95.

Succulents indoors

The ever-adaptable succulent, at home in the landscape or in a container, is equally able to thrive indoors. This ability to grow under such a wide variety of circumstances is good news for gardeners of all persuasions. The succulent's adaptability to an indoor climate makes it possible for everyone to enjoy growing cacti and other succulents, especially apartment and condominium dwellers.

Below: Large specimens aren't required when collecting succulents. Here an entire collection in small containers takes center stage on brick-and-board shelves.

Below: Tropical succulents in hanging containers share this outdoor living area with pots of South African pelargoniums, creating a lush, relaxing spot.

The uses for succulents in the interior landscape are as varied and creative as the plants themselves. If you have a collection that is still young and small, it can be easily accommodated on one or more windowsills. A row of cacti in the window over the kitchen sink can do a lot to improve the view (and your attitude) while washing the dishes.

When your collection expands beyond the available windowsills, simply go vertical and install a row of narrow shelves in the widow frame. Because many succulents tend to stay small or are slow-growing and because they can be purchased as miniature-growing species (many rebutias, mammillarias, and fraileas), they are ideally suited to growing in limited spaces.

A desert in your living room

Larger specimens can be used in a variety of ways in your interior landscape. Just as pots of cacti can be sunk into the ground outdoors to give the feeling of a permanent, natural landscape, containerized succulents can also be used to simulate an interior desertscape.

A simple plywood box, painted and lined with heavy plastic film can accommodate your succulent collection. An inch or two of pebbles at the bottom of the box will provide sufficient drainage. Surrounding the pots with a porous material — potting soil, perlite or vermiculite — and adding a layer of builder's sand or pea gravel as a top dressing will give it the finishing touch. The pots are easily removed for deep watering; allow the bulk of the water to drain off before replac-

A sunny south-facing window is a perfect place for this cactus collection.

A large strawberry pot is easily transformed into a container for succulents.

Above: Baskets of Sedum morganianum *(donkey's-tail) hanging under a tree.*

Right: A collection of cacti and a Dracaena deremensis *combine to create a distinctive interior landscape.*

Stand-up mirrors provide a dramatic backdrop for large cacti specimen in this apartment living room.

Succulents can improve the looks of any room. Here they brighten a kitchen.

ing the pots in the landscape box. This box design makes indoor landscaping a convenient reality, and advances your collection beyond the status of ordinary house plants.

Succulent sculpture

Because succulents, especially cacti, are such structurally dramatic plants, they can be used as living sculpture throughout your home. There's something special about a tall, slender, cactus standing sentinel in a corner, or, grouped with other succulents to provide a striking accent for a room's decor.

Be sure to keep this architectural quality in mind when shopping for succulents and cacti you are going to grow inside your home. Because their shapes are so distinctive, it's important to consider if the plants will suit the existing space and furnishings.

Light on the subject

The light requirements are another important consideration when choosing succulents for your indoor landscape. As a general rule, most cacti and many other succulents require bright light with some direct sun. However, there are succulents that prefer moderate amounts of light, for example, epiphyllums and many haworthias. Check the plant's specific requirements in the cultural charts pages 94, 95, and plan your selections and placements accordingly.

Artificial light gardening

Keep artificial lighting in mind if you find you don't have enough natural light, or if your collection begins to outgrow the well-lighted areas in your home or apartment.

Artificial lights can either be used as a supplement to existing natural light, or as the sole source of light for your plants. If you find your large specimens need just a few more hours of sun each day to stay healthy, they can be spotlighted with an incandescent Gro-light in the evenings. This not only gives the plants their needed light, but the lighting "spotlights" your plants, making them more prominent in your decorating scheme, giving you a chance to admire them in the evenings.

Artificial alone

Perhaps, because of surrounding buildings or tall trees, your apartment or home just doesn't get very much sunlight at all. Don't give up. We met two avid growers who have over

3,000 plants in their New York City apartment, and they are *all* grown under artificial lights. And if that isn't amazing enough, all 3,000 are growing in a spare bedroom!

This particular light garden, owned by Harriet and Murray Goldmintz, has evolved into one of the best in the country. Mr. Goldmintz began growing his succulents and cacti long before artificial light gardening was popular and has gained much valuable knowledge from his experiences.

The Goldmintzes use full-spectrum Vita-Lite fluorescent tubes, placed approximately 6 inches away from the plants, and burned for 16 hours each day. Because the plants are given such regular cultural treatment, their growth is very consistent and compact.

The Goldmintz's growing room is a perfect example of space utilization and organization. The plants are arranged around the edges of the room, on adjustable brick-and-board shelving, with storage of materials under the shelves.

Even if you don't have an entire bedroom to give over to your collection, you can still grow an amazing number of plants in one space with the help of artificial lighting.

The most important considerations in putting together your artificial light garden are the kinds of lights you plan to use. They should be full spectrum. Ordinary lamps, whether incandescent or fluorescent, do not emit the same wave lengths of light that are needed by plants for healthy growth. Incandescent bulbs have the advantage of being easier to install in already-existing fixtures and have the possibility of being used as spotlights, but their disadvantages are several: they are more expensive to burn, they do not last as long as fluorescent tubes and the heat they give off can damage plants.

It is cheaper in the long run to invest in fluorescent tubes and balasts (the fixtures that hold the tubes). While many other kinds of plants will be perfectly happy under standard fluorescent tubes, the full-spectrum types (Vita-Lite, Gro-Lux Wide Spec-

trum, and Naturescent/Optima, among other brands) are required for maximum plant development.

Indoor culture

Whether your indoor succulents are grown in natural light or under fluorescent or incandescent bulbs, culture is relatively easy. Fast-draining soil is all-important, as are light and frequent feedings with a good fertilizer. Container-grown succulents, especially those in small or clay pots, will require more frequent waterings than those grown in large pots or in the ground.

This variation in watering needs results partly from the relatively hot, dry environment inside most homes. While the heat and low humidity will not damage most succulents as they would a humidity-loving fern, succulents in their natural habitat go through a period of dormancy induced by a drop in temperature.

So don't be afraid to open the window for some fresh, cool air, or feel compelled to keep your home or apartment heated for your plants.

Cryptanthus of the bromeliad family is sometimes grown as a tropical succulent. This collection, spotlighted under grow-lights.

A miniature succulent landscape grows under artificial lights.

A spare bedroom houses this succulent collection. Over 3,000 plants line the shelves, all grown under artificial lights.

Succulents for special situations

As a collector, you might find succulents are suitable for many landscape situations, both indoors and outdoors. In order to help you choose the appropriate genera and species, we have assembled a list of circumstances and recommended plants. As you read through these listings, it will become apparent that many plants are versatile enough to be suitable for several situations. Keep in mind that these selections are subjective. There are many other plants that you will find effective in your own landscaping needs.

Outdoor landscaping

LARGE LANDSCAPE SPECIMENS

Aeonium tabuliforme
Aeonium arboreum 'Atropurpureum'
Agave americana
Agave attenuata
Cereus peruvianus
C. peruvianus 'Monstrosus'
Dasylirion longifolium
Dudleya brittonii
Pachycereus pecten-aboriginum
(All of the above are frost-tender plants)

GROUND COVERS
Lampranthus filicaulis
Lampranthus productus
Lampranthus spectabilis
Sedum x rubrotinctum

Recommended for steep slopes:
Drosanthemum floribundum
Drosanthemum hispidum
Malephora crocea
Malephora c. purpureo-crocea

Winter-hardy ground covers:
Sedum anglicum
Sedum brevifolium
Sedum dasyphyllum
Sedum spurium
Sempervivum tectorum
Sempervivum hybrids

ROCK GARDENS
Agave victoriae-reginae
Aloe aristata
Aloe brevifolia
Echeveria derenbergii
Echeveria x imbricata
Mammillaria geminispina
Mammillaria prolifera

Winter-hardy plants:
Sedum species
Sempervivum species

Container landscaping

CONTAINER SPECIMENS
Agave victoriae-reginae
Astrophytum myriostigma
Dudleya brittonii
Echeveria hybrids
Echinocactus grusonii
Echinocactus platyacanthus
Euphorbia flanagenii 'cristata'
Ferocactus latispinus

HANGING-BASKET PLANTS
Aporocactus flagelliformis
Ceropegia woodii
Crassula 'Jade Necklace'
Epiphyllum species and hybrids
Graptopetalum paraguayense
Hylocereus undatus
Rhipsallis capilliformis
Schlumbergera hybrids
Sedum morganianum
Senecio herreianus
Senecia rowleyanus

House plants

HANGING PLANTS
Ceropegia woodii
Rhipsallis capilliformis
Hoya species
Senecio rowleyanus

SMALL-GROWING
WINDOWSILL SPECIMENS
Astrophytum asterias
Astrophytum myriostigma
Cephalocereus senilis
Epithelantha micromeris
Lithops species
Lobivia binghamiana
Mammillaria species
Pelecyphora aselliformis
Rebutia species
Schlumbergera species and hybrids

Artificial light gardens

Adromischus species
Astrophytum myriostigma
Euphorbia species — small-growing
Haworthia species
Mammillaria species

Bonsai subjects

Adenium species
Bursera species
Cycas revoluta
Fouquieria columnaris
Jatropha cathartica
Pachypodium windsorii
Portulacaria afra
Trichodiadema bulbosum

Particularly interesting forms

Crassula 'Moonglow'
Dinteranthus puberulus
Euphorbia obesa
Fenestraria rhopalophylla
Hatiora salicornioides

Lapidaria margaretae
Lithops species
Melocactus species

Colorful foliage

Cotyledon ladysmithiensis
Kalanchoe tomentosa
Pachyphytum 'Blue Haze'
X Pachyveria varieties
Senecio haworthii

Attractive and plentiful flowers

Chamaecereus sylvestri and hybrids
Echeveria species and hybrids
Euphorbia milii
Gymnocalycium species
Kalanchoe blossfeldiana
Lobivia species
Mammillaria species
Pelargonium echinatum
Rhipsallis species
Rebutia species
Schlumbergera species and hybrids

Mail-order sources

On the facing page (page 23) you will find a list of mail-order nurseries. Mail-order nurseries make it convenient for collectors all over the United States and Canada to buy a wide variety of high quality plants. These mail-order nurseries, and the informative catalogs they provide, are a real help to collectors who do not have the advantage of a nearby nursery or garden center. On the whole, they are general succulent nurseries. If they specialize in one genera or another, we have noted their speciality below the address.

Succulents received from mail-order nurseries often arrive potted in lightweight soil mixes specially prepared for shipping and handling. The soil mix is adequate to maintain the plant during the shipping process, but some plants may need to be repotted in another rooting medium before they become a part of your permanent collection. For complete information on potting see the Culture and Propagation chapter, starting on page 85.

One final note: The mail-order nurseries are numbered from 1 to 37. These numbers correspond to the numbers which appear in the gallery chapter (pages 49-83) after the recommended species. We have indicated specific catalog availability on all recommended species with exception of those species which are wdely available.

Mail-order nurseries

The following is a list of thirty-seven mail-order nurseries. Most of them have a large selection of both cacti and other succulents. Specializations in one or two genera or families has been noted below the nursery's name and address.

1. Seaborn del Dios Nursery
   Route 3, P.O. Box 455
   Escondido, Ca. 92025
   Specializing in bromeliads and cycads.

2. Barnet Cactus Garden
   1104 Meadowview Drive
   Bossier City, La. 71111

3. Desert Dan's
   Nursery Seed Company
   Minitola, New Jersey 08341

4. Intermountain Cactus
   1478 North 750 East
   Kaysville, Utah 84037
   Specializing in opuntias and other winter-hardy plants.

5. Modlins Cactus Gardens
   2416 El Corto
   Vista, Ca. 92083

6. Nature's Curiosity Shop
   2560 Ridgeway Drive
   National City, Ca. 92050
   A large selection of succulents and bromeliads.

7. Kirkpatrick's Rare & Unusual Cactus
   27785 De Anza Street
   Barstow, Ca. 92311
   A very large selection of unusual cacti and other succulents.

8. Howard Wise
   3710 June Street
   San Bernardino, Ca. 92405
   Dealing exclusively in cacti.

9. Helen's Cactus
   2205 Mirasol Ave.
   Brownsville, Texas 78520

10. Collector's Succulents
    Cathryn Mangold
    P.O. Box 1998
    Rancho Santa Fe, Ca. 92067

11. California Epi Center
    P.O. Box 2474
    Van Nuys, Ca. 91404
    Specializing in epiphyllums and other tropical cacti.

12. North Jersey Bromeliads
    P.O. Box 181
    Alpine, New Jersey 07620
    Specializing in bromeliads.

13. Ben Haines
    1902 Lane
    Topeka, Kansas 66604
    Specializing in winter-hardy cacti and other succulents.

14. Hawk's Nursery
    2508 E. Vista Way
    Vista, Ca. 92083
    Specializing in epiphyllums.

15. Cactus by Mueller
    10411 Rosedale Hwy.
    Bakersfield, Ca. 93308

16. Jessup's Cactus Nursery
    P.O. Box 327
    Aromas, Ca. 95004

17. Walther's Exotic House Plants
    RD 3, Box 30
    Catskill, New York 12414
    Specializing in bromeliads, cacti and other succulents.

18. Loehman's Cactus Patch
    8014 Howe Street
    P.O. Box 871
    Paramount, Ca. 90723

19. Oakhill Gardens
    Route 3, Box 87
    Dallas, Oregon 97338
    Specializing in sedums and sempervivums.

20. Henrietta's Nursery
    1345 North Brawley
    Fresno, Ca. 93711
    A large selection of cacti and succulents, including hybridized schlumbergergas.

21. Scotts Valley Cactus
    5311 Scotts Valley Drive
    Scotts Valley, Ca. 95066

22. Fernwood Plants
    P.O. Box 268
    Topanga, Ca. 90290

23. Cactus Gem Nursery
    10092 Mann Drive
    Cupertino, Ca. 95014

24. K & L Cactus Nursery
    12712 Stockton Bl.
    Galt, Ca. 95632

25. Singer's Growing Things
    6385 Enfield Ave.
    Reseda, Ca. 91335
    A selection of unusual succulents, including stapeliads, mesembs and cycads.

26. Linda Goodman's Sun Plants
    P.O. Box 20014
    Riverside, Ca. 92516

27. Desert Plant Company
    P.O. Box 880
    Marfa, Texas 79843
    Specializing in cacti.

28. Grote's Cactus Gardens
    13555 So. Leland Road
    Oregon City, Ore. 97045

29. Sturtevant's Cactus and Succulent Nursery
    Arlington, Ore. 97812

30. Beahm's Epiphyllum Gardens
    2686 Paloma Street
    Pasadena, Ca. 91107
    Specializing in epiphyllums, rhipsalis, and hoyas.

31. Abbey Gardens
    176 Toro Canyon Road
    Carpinteria, Ca. 93013
    A large selection of succulents, including cacti and other specialty plants.

32. Lakeview Gardens
    Route 3, Box 447
    Escondido, Ca. 92025
    Specializing in bromeliads.

33. Whitestone Gardens, Ltd.
    The Cactus Houses
    Sutton-under-Whitestonecliff
    Thirsk, Yorkshire,
    England YO 72PZ

34. Ed Storms, Lithops
    4223 Pershing
    Fort Worth, Texas 76107
    An extensive selection of lithops and other mesembs. Also some succulent specialty plants.

35. Ashwood Specialty Plants
    4629 Centinela Ave.
    Los Angeles, Ca. 90066
    A large selection including tropical cacti and bromeliads.

36. Grigsby Cactus Gardens
    2326 & 2354 Bella Vista
    Vista, Ca. 92083

37. "Cycadia"
    17337 Chase St.
    Northridge, Ca. 91324
    Specializing in rare African species.

Other special addresses

If you have difficulty locating pumice through a local merchant, try writing to the distributor:

American Pumice Products, Inc.
221 West Dyer Road
Santa Ana, CA. 92707

Membership in the Cactus and Succulent Society and subscriptions to their journal are available from:

Cactus and Succulent
Society Journal,
Abbey Garden Press
P.O. Box 3010
Santa Barbara, CA 93105

Playful plants

Besides being easy to grow, water-thrifty, and eye-pleasing, succulents have another side to their nature. They're just plain fun to have around. Here are some ideas to get you started on enjoying your collection — in your garden or your home, in clay pots or specially made containers, as a few playful plants or a huge collection.

Walk down the aisle of any nursery that carries cacti and other succulents and see if you can get out without buying one. They're small, they're irresistible and you may find yourself saying, "What are a few pennies for so much fun?" It's probably the way many collectors got started, and for you this may be just the beginning.

One of the first things you may catch yourself doing is seeing something in these plants other than what they actually are. Many of their common names came about because they reminded someone of something else — bishop's-cap *(Astrophytum myriostigma)* for example, on page 7, or string-of-beads *(Senecio rowleyanus)*. Sometimes it takes your imagination — a hairy little cactus may remind you of a troll.

Donkey's-tail (Sedum morganianum) fills basket on back of terra cotta donkey planter from Mexican import shop. Neutral bisque serves as background for this handsome slow-growing succulent.

Only the beginning

In this chapter we will show you just a few of the possibilities that await you when you bring that first plant home. We give suggestions for choosing just the right container for the single plant, move on to suggestions for bringing collections of plants together in dish gardens, and tell you how to handle your garden trimmings — we call it recycling. At the end of the chapter we'll report our conversations with several collectors — people who have collected cacti and other succulents as a hobby — and tell you how they've handled, propagated, displayed, and enjoyed their plants.

Bringing your first plant home is only part of the fun. The other part is finding just the right pot. Cacti and other succulents rarely need coddling. Porous soil, good drainage, filtered sun is all they ask — and a minimum amount of water. So any container you see that will hold a little soil and offers good drainage can be pressed into service with happy results. You

are a sort of marriage broker, introducing just the right plant to just the right pot.

Whereas one plant to one pot is more a matter of finding a good one-to-one relationship, the dish garden is a matter of finding a congenial collection of plants (a blend of form and color pleasing to the eye) and then combining them in a situation or container that will show them off to their best advantage. Dish garden containers vary considerably. We will show, for example, the use of a cast-off garden fountain and an old basket chair.

Some succulents are so prolific — *Sedum spathulifolium,* for example, or *Crassula argentia* — that you have to keep trimming them back before they take over the garden path. Instead of throwing the cuttings out, start more plants for your friends or use them for temporary table or other home decorations. It's amazing how long these temporary plants will last. "Temporary" can mean months as far as succulents are concerned.

On top of wall-hung cabinet, hen-and-chicks (Echeveria x imbricata) *nestle among ceramic hens to add playful note to kitchen.*

Plant puns

Succulents lend themselves with remarkable ease to a play on words — we call them "plant puns."

Our terra-cotta donkey is planted with donkey's tail *(Sedum morgania-num).* The stonelike head of a woman done in clay is planted with a succulent called Medusa's-head, which resembles the snakes that supplanted the hair of Medusa in Greek mythology. The succulent is aptly named *Euphorbia caput-medusae.*

These are just to start you thinking. More will come to mind as you become involved in this fascinating world.

Euphorbia milii, *commonly known as crown-of-thorns, makes an appropriate planting in this container.*

Graptopetalum paraguayense, *often called ghost plant, is perfectly suited to a unique ceramic planter, adorns this lady, framing her face in an Easter bonnet of pearl gray.*

Medusa's-head (Euphorbia caput-medusae) *springs from stone head.*

What do you see?

As we've said, cacti and other succulents lend themselves well to puns. On this and the next page, you'll find just a sampling of another of their playful characteristics — that of reminding us of something else. You'll discover many more examples for yourself. As you look through catalogs, or browse the nurseries, your eyes will become trained to watch for the playful possibilities of cacti and other succulents.

Often the something you see can be emphasized or played up by a special container or reinforced by its surroundings. A good example of

What looks like a roly-poly Teddy bear with fur-trimmed cap is actually the cactus Mammillaria tetracantha *with pups forming its finger.*

Hot air balloons are really Euphorbia obesa, *also known as baseball plant.*

Our Aeonium arboreum atropurpureum 'cristata' *resembles a rooster.*

this is our owl-eyes *(Mammillaria parkinsonii)* whose stare is repeated by a ceramic owl.

The surprise element in succulents and cacti is largely responsible for their fascination. In maturity, some are very different in shape and form from the young plant. And the amount of light in which they're grown can make a big difference in foliage color.

Many strange shapes are caused by the natural evolution of the plants. Take the rock-resembling lithops for example, at the top of page 25. Nature evolved a way of protecting them from predators, reducing them to two leaves, with a coloration that allowed them to blend in with their native

Blast-off immediately comes to mind in time of space exploration. It's really Aeonium urbicum. *Backlighting brings pink glow to the edges of the leaves.*

The geometric structure of Crassula *'Moonglow' recalls a Japanese pagoda.*

habitat. They hug the ground, their surfaces barely uncovered, hardly discernible from the rocky ground in which they live.

A plant inclined to have unstable genes might do crazy things. Some horticulturists believe that the crests on our rooster plant, above, may be the result of early injury, a puncture wound or knife cut, that caused the growth pattern to be altered. These oddballs can be found in almost any family, including cactus, although some families are more prone than others to producing bizarre mutations. They probably start out all right, but something happens along the way to disturb the normal growth pattern.

In addition to strange shapes, you will find occasional deviations from the color norm with some very beautiful foliage variegations being produced. These oddities in a species are called "sports." Theories to account for these deviations range from a virus to freak mutation in the genes.

A strange plant may have perfectly normal offsets. To maintain a crest, for example, you should remove it and reroot it if the plant shows

signs of returning to normalcy. Or you can remove the normal offsets to avoid reducing the crested form. It is best to go to a specialty nursery to find these mutations. On rare occasions a sharp-eyed collector can pick one up at the super market; spotting the beginnings of an interesting deviation which other shoppers, not so knowledgeable, will reject. A collector knows that it may take more growth before the true character and fascination of the strange mutation will be evident.

Owl-eyes are formed by the inherent spine arrangement of Mammillaria parkinsonii.

Be creative with containers

Containers line the walls of nurseries, they line the walls of import stores. You find them in supermarkets, you find them in hardware stores. In fact, they're nearly everywhere you look. Almost everything has to go into something, and it's certainly true of plants. This whole chapter is as much about containers as it is about plants; the two are so inseparable.

Containers come in all sorts of materials: glazed and unglazed ceramic, stoneware, metalware, plastic, woven grasses, wood; even rocks and shells offer pockets for soil.

The important thing to remember when you choose a container for a succulent plant of any kind is that it should provide good drainage. Most containers come with a drainage hole; if it is too small, you can enlarge it with a handrasp or stickleback drill. If the container doesn't have any drainage hole, you can make one yourself. Use an electric drill with a special bit for ceramics or glass, a standard bit for wood. And if it's not convenient to drill a hole, you can layer gravel on the bottom of the pot, set your plant in a clay pot inside the container and water *very carefully* so the bottom of the pot doesn't rest in water. This method also enables you to raise the level of the plant to where you want it.

Playful collection of turtle planters is also perfect home for this succulent collection.

The tortoise and the hare — Haworthia tessallata followed by Cephalocereus senilis.

Worth study for masterly matching of plant to pot; collected over the years, ceramic containers made by a former art teacher and her students.

Curve of Aloe suprafoliata echoes line and color of a simple snail planter.

Succulents grow anywhere: at an Oregon nursery, worn boots hold sempervivum.

St. Francis planter in shallow bird bath; has gravel layer to solve drainage problem.

Handmade containers with aquatic theme on the deck of an Oregon home.

The advantage of plastic, glazed ceramic, or metal is that each will cut down on watering. Such containers are especially good for growing plants if you're frequently away from home.

Choose the right pot

Your container should be large enough to allow the roots of the plant a little spreading room. As a general rule, select a pot one or two inches larger than the diameter of a rosette succulent; a container half as wide as a vertical plant is tall. Size is important. A small pot dries out rapidly, too large a pot will hold too much soil to dry out properly. With these guidelines in mind, choosing a pot for a special plant is a little easier.

Three bowls: inexpensive terra-cotta planter holds triumvirate of succulents, each plant a recent cutting from mature specimen.

Sedum spathulifolium 'pruinosum' is rooted in planter on other side of fence.

Or seven bowls: handsome handmade pottery with multicups on pedestal base hold deep maroon Aeonium x 'Schwartzkopf,' Haworthia cuspidata, *and* crassula *species.*

Senecio rowleyanus on neck; lap of Sedum spathulifolium for roguish lady.

A bamboo birdcage, purchased at an Oriental import shop, makes an appropriate home for graceful trailing succulents like Senecio herreianus.

Rosettes of Echeveria elegans *make an uncluttered planting for strawberry jar.*

Drawer of old coffee grinder holds bonsai pot of Mammillaria elongata, *surrounded by a collar of its own babies.*

Keep in mind the structure of the plant; is it best when seen from above, or is it more interesting at eye level? Is it a tree type that would be more enhanced by an architectural setting? Cascading succulents, for example, do well in hanging baskets. Good air circulation keeps them thriving and they can be viewed from all angles.

We had fun bringing tillandsias up to eye level. These are members of the bromeliad family, feathery little air plants that use their roots for a perch, but live and breathe through their leaves. You'll see them on page 37.

Once the guidelines for culture have been met, you can choose your pot for humor. Or, you can choose it for aesthetics: color can enhance the foliage; line and form can enhance the growth structure. Look at the whole — plant and container — as a piece of sculpture. If you look at them that way, what you might consider expensive as a plant, could seem inexpensive as a piece of sculpture.

A careful study of the planter-plant grouping in our first photograph, page 28, shows particularly how a plant can be matched to its planter. These pots are all handmade. You'll find many more examples of hand-made pots scattered through the chapter. Pot-making is a rewarding art; you can make a pot to order for a special plant, or reverse the order, choosing a plant for a pot you've already made. And if you don't have any talent along these lines, you needn't despair. The world is full of

Donkey's-tail (Sedum morganianum) *spills down flutes of an old bird bath.*

Above: Abandoned urn and sundial: reddish-black Aeonium x 'Schwartzkopf' *mark the quarter hours.* Sedum rubro-tinctum *fills hours in between.*

Right: Miniature hibachi used for hors d'oeuvres holds small collection of cacti and other succulents.

Gate stone: Imagination rock from Mexico has natural planting pockets, good drainage for succulents.

talented people eager to find buyers, and you'll find very special pots, particularly if you haunt craft shops and craft shows.

Dish gardens

While many succulents beg to be singled out, others might like to join a group. If you find yourself collecting more plants than you know what to do with and containers are running short, you can group your plants quite successfully in dish gardens. Cacti and other succulents are ideal for dish gardens because many are basically small and they grow slowly. Once established, they don't outgrow the pot right away.

The important thing about dish gardens is to choose plants that like

Lap of old basket chair destined for refuse pile offers perfect drainage, an unusual place to plant varied succulents.

Above: Drawers of small utility box serve as a temporary display for succulents.

Right: Study in color: plastic dishpan in New Jersey greenhouse is packed with lithops. They like the deep root room.

the same environment, need the same amount of watering at the same time and show the same response to light. You can build miniature landscapes using all cacti, or other succulents, or a combination of the two. In this endeavor, you can consider yourself an adoption agency, choosing just the right members to add to a family group.

Other elements (a round flat stone, a twisted piece of driftwood) can be introduced for added interest. Combining texture and color is fun and dish gardens offer the opportunity to use a wide variety of other elements in addition to plants. The tiered dish garden is a favorite. Here we show saucers at right, a tiered fountain below.

The bonsai look

In this chapter we also cover the use of bonsai pots for containers. See page 33. These are often more expensive than the ordinary pot, but sometimes the simplicity of their design is just what you need. The root conformation and growth pattern of some succulents is very reminiscent of the true Japanese bonsai. The succulent, although relatively young, can be pinched and trimmed to suggest a traditional bonsai. In a

Five identical terra-cotta pots, each planted with different materials, have distinct personalities, group together nicely on a green lawn.

A miniature scene in a single-layer dish garden uses wood, stone and a grouping of complementary succulents.

Great variety is possible with repeated shapes; use standard pots, oversized saucers and varied succulents.

Diminishing sizes of clay bowls each planted with shades of green succulents.

Dish gardening goes vertical. What used to be a three-tiered fountain is now a graceful planter for a collection of cacti and other succulents, a pleasing accent in a patio corner.

A single-layer garden uses wood, stone and a grouping of complementary succulents.

bonsai pot, it becomes a truly eye-arresting plant.

Bonsai succulents, while not true bonsai, have the same feeling as the traditional Japanese miniatures.

The pot should provide a contrast in line — a tall plant in an elongated bowl, for example. Don't worry about the length of the plant's roots; if covered with soil, they will grow as well spread out horizontally as reaching downward. Plant as you would any succulent, but you can mound the soil up around the stem, then give the surface a good gravel mulch. This is important as roots dry out quickly in a shallow pot. Even with the mulch, if the pot is placed in full sun to bring out foliage color, you might have to water every day. If you trim or pinch to enhance a shape, remember that growth will frequently be stopped at this spot forever. Later, it is best to nip new and unwanted growth immediately to avoid scarring.

Some special care

To water without disturbing the mulch, set the pot up to its rim in a pan of water and let it soak until the surface of the mulch is damp. Always let a bonsai succulent dry out a little between waterings.

Crested Sedum dendroideum *is well displayed in a bonsai pot with river stones.*

Deep blue of bonsai pot enhances color variation in Haworthia fasciata 'variegata.'

Repotted several times to encourage gnarled growth: Trichodiadema bulbosum.

Reddish tips along branches are spines on an old looking Euphorbia squarrosa.

Another Trichodiadema bulbosum *has been kept to miniature size in a tiny pot.*

Handcrafted display stand, designed and built by Joseph Rubio, is a copy of a Japanese bonsai stand, used here for showing off a collection of interesting bonsai succulents.

Centerpiece for dining room table: glowing candles, a favorite sea shell and floating rosettelike succulents in an acrylic salad bowl.

Don't overwater. The thick roots of *Trichodiadema bulbosum,* page 33, serve as a good-sized storage tank. This thick stock is best achieved if you don't overwater.

Feed infrequently, just often enough to keep the plant healthy. You don't want vigorous growth; it would soon outgrow its pot. To keep bonsai succulents indoors for any length of time, place them under a wide-spectrum Gro-Lux fluorescent light.

Playful and prolific

We can't guarantee that your garden will someday be overflowing with succulents, but if that day should come, on this and the next three pages you will find some suggestions on how to handle the situation.

Some succulents seem to grow and spread very quickly. This is probably just an illusion. They require so little care that you're not aware that they're taking over until suddenly there they are, encroaching on the pavement or pushing aside neighboring plants. This is particularly true if they are planted in a spot where they catch the same amount of water that nonsucculent plants require.

Party favors

When you prune them, don't toss the trimmings away. They can be used in a variety of ways. Perhaps one of the most satisfying and rewarding is to pot them up and give them to friends. You might use them, for example, as party favors. What friend wouldn't love to leave a luncheon or a dinner party with a live plant in hand? If you run out of time, you needn't pot them up, but simply give several cuttings in an attractive container with verbal instructions for their planting and care. (You may make a succulent convert!) And even if they never get planted, they will last a long time.

Table decorations

Try floating them among candles as we did in the centerpiece on this page. A large acrylic salad bowl was filled with water to a depth of 2 inches and the candles placed upright, attached to the bowl with florist's clay. If some of the succulents should sink, it only adds to the three-dimensional effect.

You can also use them as simple table decorations.

We have a friend who took an attractive rectangular basket and filled it with 4-inch pots of succulents to use as a one-time centerpiece. But you may use your trimmings unplanted also — to rim a saucer as in the Mexican-like setting of our table, which uses terra-cotta pots and saucers with a bit of yarn and leftover trimmings of *Sedum rubrotinctum.*

Household accents

We also show several ways to use trimmings to brighten up other areas of the house: *Graptopetalum paraguayense* stuck on the tips of skewers, interspersed with strawflowers for contrast, arranged in a chemical flask as an instant bouquet for a guest bath; or the conch shell book end, planted as this one is, but just as attractive if the trimmings are tucked into the opening in the shell.

Bouquet of Graptopetalum paraguayense *on skewers with bright strawflowers, assembles quickly to brighten bathroom corner.*

Conch shell bookend frames planting of Sedum rubrotinctum *and* S. spathulifolium.

Many things will come to mind as temporary containers. You will find a large source of them around the house: plastic bottle caps from laundry softener bottles, bulk wine bottles, men's toiletries, spray cans of all sorts, the panty-hose containers mentioned on page 36. Or, you can pick up shells at the beach and perhaps find wind- and water-eroded rocks with built-in planting holes for a little soil and a succulent rosette.

Fernbark plant stakes, which come in 2 x 2-inch poles, can be cut into blocks and a hole hollowed out on one side to hold soil. In some nurseries and hardware stores that carry craft supplies, you might find fernbark balls, like the one we show here in our table setting. (You may have to ask at several places; they are not too easy to find.) If you have good-sized-diameter bamboo in your garden, you can take the culms, saw them just below a nodule and make a tiny pot. Instead of soil, use sphagnum moss, tucked into a tiny container to hold moisture and secure the plant.

Holiday helper

Expendable cuttings and temporary containers are particularly useful for holiday decorations. The rosette type succulents, best viewed from above, gain added sparkle from the head of a straight pin used to

Little baskets planted with trimmings from garden fill large basket as centerpiece, also grace each place setting as party favors.

Arrangement of pots and saucers, reminiscent of a Mexican hat, hold garden trimmings; small saucers for candles repeat theme.

Patio breakfast table decorated with fernbark blocks and fernbark centerpiece, holding cuttings of Aeonium haworthii *and* Echeveria pulvinata.

Clam shell holds cuttings of Sedum rubrotinctum *and* Echeveria x imbricata; *babies hold haworthias.*

Substitute succulents for fresh flowers or bows in package wraps. Decoration in foreground is planted in baby-food jar top.

Scrap-wood tree covered with felt; red and green succulent trimmings pinned in place.

affix them to the box top. Notice the green of *Aeonium haworthii* and red of *Crassula 'Campfire'* which are pinned to our Christmas tree, at left. The silvery ornaments, below, were made from panty-hose containers, hung from yarn, and filled with succulent trimmings. An electric drill was used to make three equidistant holes in the half-egg shapes, the yarn threaded through the holes, and knotted.

Start the wreath (below) several months ahead of time so it will be filled in by Christmas. Soak the moss in water, wring it out and pack it tightly into the wire frame; it will contract when it dries. Pick slow-growing succulents that stay small. Remove their leaves so you have about 1½ inches of stem to tuck into holes made in the moss with a pencil or chopstick. After the wreath is planted, lay it in partial shade so the plants will root. Water well, but let it dry out between waterings. Because the moss has no nutrients, feed it once every two weeks with a weak solution of liquid fertilizer. Water it just before you bring it indoors. The wreath will last about a week inside; mist it if the foliage seems to be drying out.

The importance of perspective

Up to this point, we've talked about plants viewed from above, either on the ground or in table containers. Succulents, just like many other plants, show off to advantage at eye level. By bringing them up for closer viewing, you add variety and interest to your garden landscaping. At this level the plant and the container

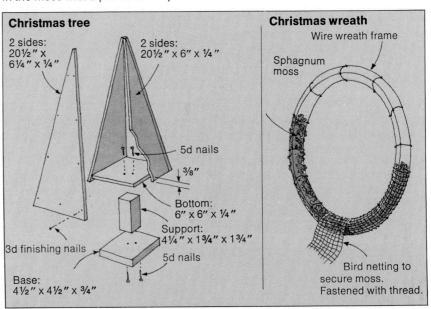

Christmas tree

2 sides: 20½" x 6¼" x ¼"

2 sides: 20½" x 6" x ¼"

5d nails

⅜"

Bottom: 6" x 6" x ¼"

Support: 4¼" x 1¾" x 1¾"

3d finishing nails

5d nails

Base: 4½" x 4½" x ¾"

Christmas wreath

Wire wreath frame

Sphagnum moss

Bird netting to secure moss. Fastened with thread.

Design: Florence Sullivan

Above: Base for Christmas wreath is sphagnum moss packed in wire frame, supporting succulents in many shades of green, accented with a red bow.

Left: To decorate tree or branch, silvery orbs hold garden trimmings, hang from brightly colored yarn.

become more important. The donkey on our opening page stands at eye level on a terraced retaining wall, the hen-and-chicks are high in a kitchen, the Medusa's-head and ghost plant are on garden pedestals.

We've reserved the little tillandsias especially for this eye-level section. These fetching plants, members of the bromeliad family, like good air circulation and being high where they can catch any moisture; they use their roots to hang onto things. You can mist them, if your climate is fairly moist, or dunk them in a container of water, if you live in a dry area.

We show the tillandsias in two eye-level situations, where their light, feathery appearance can be enjoyed to the fullest. They even produce small bright blooms. You can attach

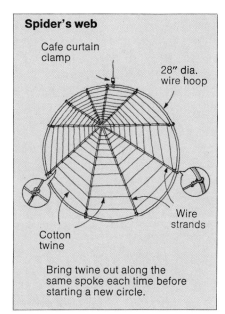

Spider's web

Cafe curtain clamp

28" dia. wire hoop

Wire strands

Cotton twine

Bring twine out along the same spoke each time before starting a new circle.

Spidery Tillandsia schiedeana *catches prey* (T. ionantha) *in string web woven inside a wire hoop knotted on wire spokes.*

them to almost any surface by almost any means (glue, nails, thread).

Their leaf pattern lends itself well to our spider web. The little clusters were wrapped in place with thread, eventually their roots will curl around the string of the spider web. On the spoon mobile, below, where they were attached with white glue, staples, even a small nail, they will root themselves to the wooden bowls.

Wooden planting pockets

The handsome planters on page 38 were designed by George L. Schmidt of Torrance, California, whose garden you see on page 45. Mr. Schmidt uses scraps of cedar or redwood grapestake fencing.

To make your own, take even lengths of 3- or 4-inch-wide scrap-wood; the length will depend on how

Simple mobile: Bottle cap hangs in knotted sling inside embroidery hoops; each member hangs from fishing swivels.

Above: Cholla wood, stuffed with sphagnum moss, forms natural plant pockets for trimmings.

Right: Bowls of wooden spoons which hang from oval hoop, hold tillandsias which like the moist atmosphere above kitchen sink. Euphorbia milii is at left.

In tiny bedroom atrium, wood planters decorate wall, offer wide variety of succulents for close-up enjoyment.

Each one is a picture by itself; note front-to-back depth for planting pocket.

Scrap wood can also be used to make an attractive free-standing planter box.

Close-up shows color variety ranging from red to yellow-green to blue-green.

large you want your planter. These are about 15 x 15 inches. Determine your design by crisscrossing the lengths loosely on top of a solid wood backing in such a way as to create a planting pocket. Use galvanized nails to attach the first layer or two to your backing. At this point, turn the planter over and attach a galvanized wire hanger, winding it around a nail head.

Fill the planting pocket with a light soil mix of ⅓ loam, ⅓ peat moss, and ⅓ sponge rock, then cover it with a layer of damp sphagnum moss or black plastic and stretch a piece of ½-inch wire mesh over all. Finally, nail on the balance of your strips; fill any crevices with moss and plant as you wish. Leave the plaques flat for a couple of weeks until the plants root. Maintain moisture with a light spraying.

Planting a preserver

Every once in a while, we all like to splurge and do something big. Pool floats for a garden or swimming party might fill that need. Mr. Schmidt also designed these, using redwood or cedar for backing, cutting out the circles with a jig saw.

The styrofoam life preservers can be found in swim shops or some

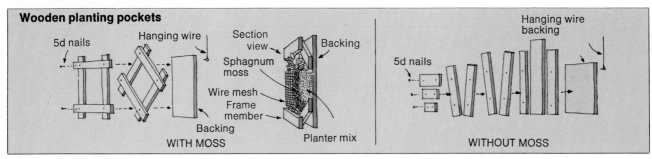

Wooden planting pockets

5d nails · Hanging wire · Section view · Backing · Sphagnum moss · Wire mesh · Frame member · Backing · Planter mix · WITH MOSS

Hanging wire backing · 5d nails · WITHOUT MOSS

Floats bob unattended in pool. Bright red of Crassula 'Campfire' stands out against the float's white background.

Swimmers position floats in preparation for festivities. Small life preservers could be used as party favors.

hardware stores. Attach them to the circles with galvanized nails, driven in from the back. Fill the center of the life preserver with a sandy mix, then arrange and plant your succulents.

Life preservers come in several sizes; the small ones shown are miniatures. You might use this size for centerpieces on tables around the pool. Or, you could leave the succulents out of the center of the small ring, shown below inside the larger ring, and use it as a floating tray for holding a glass.

Your planted life preservers need full sun, but require a minimum of care. Don't keep them permanently

in chlorinated pool water, although an occasional dunking won't do any great harm.

A vertical volcanic garden

To gain more display area for your plants, you might build a vertical Featherock planter like the one shown on the next page. The porosity of this volcanic rock makes it an ideal container for plants, particularly those requiring good drainage. It's light in weight and can be carved without the use of special tools.

This planter consists of four layered rocks, threaded onto a length of pipe. It was designed with portability in

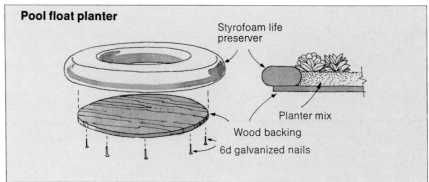

Pool float planter

Styrofoam life preserver

Planter mix

Wood backing

6d galvanized nails

Variation on a theme — small float planted inside a large float, both filled with plants.

Close-up shows attractive color and texture of these well-established plants.

Succulents fill life preservers attached to wood backing; decorate wall beside pool.

Featherock planter with succulent collection was handcrafted using ordinary household tools.

Shown before planting: each rock is threaded over length of galvanized pipe.

mind; presently, it fills a small area where gardening possibilities are limited. Later, it can be taken apart and moved to another location.

You can buy Featherock in building supply outlets that handle ornamental garden rocks and landscaping materials. Choose rocks that fit fairly well, one on top of the other, before you bring them home to build the planter. Once home, build them up again and, using a chisel, make the necessary adjustments to improve their fit. Wear gloves as you work to protect your hands, and glasses to protect your eyes.

Marking the center of each rock, disassemble and, with a 1¼-inch extension bit, drill a hole down through the center of each one to receive a 1-inch galvanized lead pipe. Insert the pipe into the bottom rock, then thread each rock layer onto the pipe.

Once the planter is assembled, decide where you want your plants and begin hollowing out planting pockets. Use an electric drill to get each hole started, then ream it out with a claw hammer or chisel. Each hole

should be large enough to receive the rootball of the plant plus a little fresh soil. On vertical rock faces, slant the hole down as much as possible so it will hold water and soil more easily.

After you finish all the holes, you are ready to plant. Start at the top and work down, rather than the other way around, to avoid spilling soil on new plantings. If needed, you can tuck sphagnum moss into the holes to help hold the soil. Water the plants in thoroughly.

Collecting for the fun of it

One thing that we've observed about collectors is that they always manage to find room for one more plant. Their gardens may be burgeoning, but by squeezing out an inch here and an inch there, they find a spot for one more little cactus or other succulent. Many have gone vertical in their gardening.

If you find yourself cramped for space, we offer one or two suggestions on how you might handle the

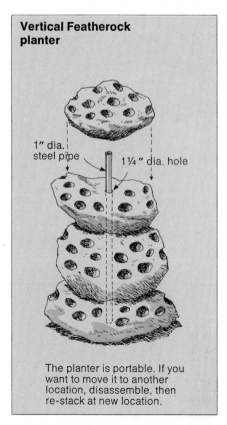

Vertical Featherock planter

1″ dia. steel pipe

1¼″ dia. hole

The planter is portable. If you want to move it to another location, disassemble, then re-stack at new location.

A do-it-yourself ten-minute easel serves as temporary display stand for new acquisitions. Flat holds Aeonium x 'Schwartzkopf.'

situation and still have the pleasure of more plants.

Take the stand at left, for example. It was put together in about ten minutes. The lumber pile yielded a three-board section of grapestake fencing, plus a 2 x 2-inch pole used at one time to support a young tree. This was nailed perpendicularly to the fencing at waist height to form a shelf, backed by a weathered strip of wood of equal length. An old nursery flat was nailed above it to suggest a picture frame for an ever-changing display. It's an ideal place to set a new plant or a flat when you bring it home from the nursery. At waist level, the pots are easy to water and fun to look at until you decide where you want to put them.

The stand below, one of several in the garden of M. R. Stern, is more elaborate and more permanent. (To see Mrs. Stern's greenhouse, turn the page.) Constructed of 1 x 8-inch redwood, the three lower tiers fit into notches in the uprights. The sketch below shows you how to put it together.

Mrs. Stern is a succulent collector, as you might have guessed. She estimates she has between five and six thousand plants in her collection. She and a friend designed her greenhouse to house choice, rare plants that didn't seem to do so well outdoors.

Four-tiered rack brings containers to workable level, offers sun and shade.

Redwood plant shelves

2"
1"
Top shelf: 1 req.
Feet: 4 req.
All material is 1" x 8" redwood.

72"
40"
16"
16"
15"
2"
4"
60"
48"
40"
18"
45°
4"
4"

All slots are 1" wide and 1½" deep.

(Lengths may be adjusted if a shorter rack is desired.)

Lower shelves: 6 req.

Upright: 2 req.

Wire braces

5d nails

Handcrafted basket-weave ceramic planters hang from edge of picnic table.

Fascinating array of pots and plants fill garden. Next year they may also hang from picnic benches as collection expands.

The framework is redwood, the walls are double-strength glass. The roof is clear corrugated plastic with a light penetration of 95 per cent; the west half of the roof and the west wall have fixed plastic panels allowing 55 per cent light penetration.

Inside, gravel is used under the plant benches on either side of a 3-foot-wide brick aisle. A high window at one end and the door at the other provide good cross-ventilation. In summer, with both open, the temperature stays around 90 degrees; in winter, with both closed, it rarely gets below 85 degrees. Neither a heater nor a fan were necessary in the coastal climate where she lives. Her workbench stands just outside the door.

Collecting as a lifestyle

Dr. and Mrs. True, owners of the garden above and at right, are also deeply committed collectors; she collects succulents, he collects bromeliads. Their enthusiasm and love for their plants is evident. They are both active in their local specialty garden clubs.

They also make their own containers as a joint endeavor. He, working at the potter's wheel, can make the large ones, she can make the smaller ones by slip casting. Whenever a plant needs a pot, she opens a cabinet door and chances are the right one is there.

They enjoy traveling and usually

bring home plants on a permit issued by the U.S. Department of Agriculture, Plant Quarantine Division. Plants must be brought in bareroot, so succulents and bromeliads make it easy to comply.

Their advice to beginners is to join a local Cactus & Succulent Society where you can meet and exchange plants with others interested in the same subject. Club libraries provide source material and, as a member of the larger national society, each club receives a monthly journal to keep you up to date in your field of special interest.

Collectors in the true sense of the word, just for the joy of discovery with plants that are beautiful or, in some cases, just unusual.

◁

Built on brick foundation, 9-foot by 12-foot greenhouse shelters choice plants; building stands 6½-feet high at eaves, 8-feet high at peak.

An ever-changing collection

Part of the joy of John and Annie Yasui's garden in Hawaii, seen at right and below right, is its changing face As soon as one plant moves out another moves in. Plants are shared with friends, neighbors, and civic organizations for their bazaars. It's busy, cluttered, loved, tended, and always changing.

It's almost exclusively a container garden. Mrs. Yasui found that plants did much better in pots than in the clay soil prevalent in her garden.

Their succulents, including cacti, are just part of a collection that ranges from vegetables to roses. Anything and everything finds a home.

Mrs. Yasui can't remember when she started collecting succulents, but feels she was one of the first residents of Hawaii to order them from California. She likes to propagate and share them now.

For her succulents, she uses mostly plastic pots so they don't have to be watered so often. For soil, she mixes volcanic black sand with a little topsoil and some sponge rock, if it's available. She feeds them only in summer, as they go into soft foliage if she feeds them in winter.

An unused clothesline becomes a hanging place for pots of succulents and cactus in this casual garden. Clothespins keep the pots in place.

Apartment dwellers use a stair landing and space under the overhang for a small succulent collection.

An old plant stand was pressed into service to handle even more containers.

A controlled collection

In direct contrast to the gardening style of the Yasuis is that of the George Schmidts in California. In their garden, plants are automatically arranged in orderly rows of color and form as though always on display.

Not a collector in the sense of having one of everything, Mr. Schmidt likes his plants to be attractive; he uses them in many planting situations and chooses them with an eye to eventually grouping them together. He formerly owned a nursery, so in retirement his home garden is a natural evolution from vocation to avocation.

The Schmidts' garden is divided into separate work areas. In addition to the plant benches shown, they use a retaining wall and steps leading from the house as display areas. Plants are moved according to their requirements for shade and sun.

A plan of their garden (below) shows how Mr. Schmidt organized it to take maximum advantage of a relatively small area.

Good planning has been followed up with good maintenance, making it possible for the Schmidts to get maximum enjoyment from their hobby.

Low benches around garden hold pots of succulents, arranged by plant family and color.

Overhead of this screened 8-foot by 12-foot-section supports plastic panels providing 35 per cent shade. Cyclone fence screening supports pots.

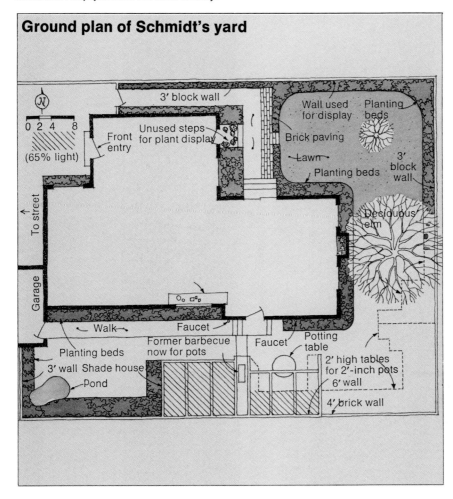

Ground plan of Schmidt's yard

0 2 4 8
(65% light)

3' block wall
Unused steps for plant display
Front entry
Wall used for display
Planting beds
Brick paving
Lawn
3' block wall
Planting beds
To street
Deciduous elm
Garage
Walk
Faucet
Former barbecue now for pots
Faucet
Potting table
2' high tables for 2'-inch pots
6' wall
Planting beds
3' wall Shade house
Pond
4' brick wall

Close-up of succulents shows owner interest in propagation. Uniform plastic pots can be packed in closely, plants need to be watered less often.

A gallery of succulents

There are enough different kinds of succulent plants to suit everyone, and everyone's lifestyle. The following gallery of over 100 genera will help you select the succulents that are right for you, and your environment.

After getting a glimpse of the many plants that are classified as succulents and all the ways they can be used, you're probably ready to go out and buy at least one plant. Perhaps to start a collection or to increase your present one. But where to start?

Try thumbing through this chapter to look at the photos and read the plant descriptions. Which kinds of plants do you find most appealing? Which are best suited to the conditions you can provide? Evaluate the available space, light, and your own cultural expertise.

In each instance, we have supplied, at least one photo of each genus mentioned in the chapter and included in the description text some appraisal of the plant's cultural needs. More detailed information can be found in the charts on pages 94, 95.

Once you've found some likely candidates, there are several ways to go buying them. As cacti and other succulents become increasingly popular, it is more likely that you'll find them in retail nurseries, plant shops — even in the supermarket.

Mail-order nurseries

You'll probably find, however, that some of the most interesting or unusual plants aren't offered through retail stores. That's when it's time to discover the mail-order specialty nurseries. We have a listing on page 23. On the whole, these are general succulent nurseries. Many others specialize in only one or two genera.

The mail-order nurseries make it possible for collectors all over the United States and Canada to buy a wide variety of high quality plants.

Each nursery puts out a catalog. Try writing away for a few of them.

The Cactus and Succulent Society

You can get lots of good information about plant availability and some expert cultural tips by joining a local chapter of the Cactus and Succulent Society or by subscribing to their journal. For information, write to the national headquarters:

Cactus and Succulent Society Journal
Abbey Garden Press
P. O. Box 3010
Santa Barbara, Ca 93105

The journal carries advertisements for many mail-order specialty nurseries. Becoming a Society member often has another advantage — it is traditional for members to exchange cuttings of their plants with one another. It can be a great way to build up a nice collection at relatively little cost, and to meet other collectors.

When your plant is nameless

If you have purchased an unidentified plant, or been given a cutting by a neighbor or friend, you'll probably be curious about that plant's name.

You'll also find it useful to know the name, because botanical nomenclature is the only reliable means of matching plant to cultural requirements. The index at the back of this book is cross-referenced for many common names and the plant's proper identification. If your plant has an unlisted common name, or no name at all, paging through our gallery of photos should help you to narrow the possibilities down to one or two genera.

How to use the gallery

Before starting to use the gallery, it might be helpful to become familiar with some of the terms we use to describe the plants. Whenever possible, we have avoided complex botanical terminology. But succulents, like any other specialized subject, require specific descriptive terms. The plant's name is one unit of that description, as we pointed out on page 7 in the introductory chapter.

A wide selection of cacti and other succulents is often available in retail nurseries.

◁
Young seedlings grow in a nursery flat.

But there's more to Botanese than a Latin name.

Each genus description in the gallery includes the following information.

Name of genus (bold type) a group of plants within a botanical family, each sharing certain common characteristics.

(jee-nuhs) pronunciation guide.

FAMILY: A large, general grouping of genera with common traits.

GROUP: A classification used only for cacti, relating to their basic types within the family.

ORIGIN: The plant's native habitat.

GENERAL DESCRIPTION: The important characteristics of the genus — stems, leaves, spines, form, color, size.

FLOWER DESCRIPTION: The shape, color, size, location and season of flowers occuring in the genus.

PROPAGATION: The means of multiplying the plant, the most common being the first mentioned.

CULTURE: The recommended general procedures and any special notes.

RECOMMENDED SPECIES: A listing of the species, based upon availability of the plant material, to include: genus initial, specie name, (previously accepted botanical nomenclature), (common names). A brief description of the specie's

Above: Globular stem of a lobivia species.
Below: Branching, columnar cereus.

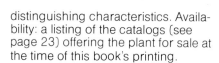
Trichocereus thelegonus has procumbent stems.

Lemaireocereus dumortieri has prominent ribs.

distinguishing characteristics. Availability: a listing of the catalogs (see page 23) offering the plant for sale at the time of this book's printing.

When you begin to read the text in the GENERAL DESCRIPTIONS and FLOWER DESCRIPTIONS, you'll probably come across some terms that are unfamiliar. With that in mind, we have compiled a vocabulary list with photos to illustrate some of the specialized words.

Vocabulary list

Apex — the top of the plant.

Areoles — the soft, cushioned base of the spines on a cactus.

Axils — the joint of two plant parts, such as tubercles or stem and leaf.

Bract — specialized leaves that are brightly colored, often mistaken for petals.

Caudex — a swollen, tuberous root system above ground level.

Cephalium — a specialized growth that forms on a cactus after it has reached maturity. It is usually wooly and is the generative point for flowers.

Clustering, clumping — a group of stems that grow together to form one mass.

Columnar — an upright, cylindrically-shaped stem.

Crested — an irregular growth that forms on some succulents.

Depressed — a stem that is wider than it is high, often with a sunken center.

Melocactus develops a cephalium.

Epiphyte — a plant that has aerial roots, used to grip trees.

Glaucous — a special powdery or waxy coating on the stems and foliage.

Globular — globelike, spherical.

Hooked spines — central spines with fishhooklike tips.

Monotypic — a genus with only one species.

Procumbent — stems that lie on the ground.

Ribs — vertical divisions of a cactus stem.

Rosettes — symmetrically arranged leaves, reminiscent of a rose.

Stapeliad — a group of plants having in common starfish-shaped flowers.

Tuber — a swollen root system

Tubercles — enlarged protuberances of a cactus stem.

Windows — an adaptive device at the top of some succulents for filtering sun.

Wool — a soft, dense, hairy growth in the areoles of cacti.

X — denotes a hybridized plant.

Above: Gymnocalycium is distinctly tubercled.
Below: Mammillaria is a clustering cactus.

Abromeitiella brevifolia

Acanthocalycium glaucum

Adenium obesum

Abromeitiella
(ah-brohm-ay-tee-*el*-ah)

FAMILY: Bromeliaceae
ORIGIN: Argentina

GENERAL DESCRIPTION:
Small mounds of triangular-shaped, thickly succulent green leaves cluster as the abromeitiella matures to a maximum of 3 to 4 feet in diameter. Tiny sharp spines are at the tips of each leaf.

FLOWER DESCRIPTION:
Greenish-yellow tubular flowers, measuring approximately 2" long, appear from the top of each leaf cluster in summer.

PROPAGATION: Cuttings.
CULTURE: General succulent culture. Easy to grow.

RECOMMENDED SPECIES:
A. brevifolia. Small mounding rosettes. Available: 1, 18, 22, 31.

Common names versus botanical names
We realize it would make it easier for many gardeners if we could list each plant by its common name, however, some plants have several common names and others have none. Botanical nomenclature has a distinct advantage in that every known plant has a name and that same name is used by horticulturists and botanists throughout the world. Because botanical names are more accurate we have listed the genera and the species in this gallery by their botanical names, in alphabetical order.

If you know a particular succulent by its common name only, please consult the list on page 96.

Acanthocalycium
(ah-*kan*-tho-kah-*lee*-see-um)

FAMILY: Cactaceae
GROUP: Echinopsis
ORIGIN: Argentina

GENERAL DESCRIPTION:
At maturity an acanthocalycium measures only 4 to 5 inches in diameter and 8 inches in height. The globular plant is green to glaucous blue, with 10 to 15 ribs and horn-colored spines 1½ inches long.

FLOWER DESCRIPTION:
Funnelform flowers are mostly white or pink, occasionally yellow. They are two inches or more in size and make a showy appearance in summer at the apex of the plant.

PROPAGATION: Seed.
CULTURE: General cactus culture. Needs to be kept fairly dry during winter, will tolerate some overwatering in summer.

RECOMMENDED SPECIES:
A. glaucum. Glaucous blue makes this attractive even when not in bloom. Flowers are yellow, spines black on columnar growth. Available. 7, 8.

A. violaceum (violet sea-urchin). Columnar to 8 inches. Lilac-colored flowers; brown spines. The most satisfactory species of the genus. Widely available.

Adenium
(ah-*dee*-nee-um)

FAMILY: Apocynaceae
ORIGIN: Socotra, tropical East Africa, South Africa

GENERAL DESCRIPTION:
Adeniums are rather strange-growing plants, each one creating its own sculptural design. The base, or caudex, varies from gray to pale brown and the stem is fleshy. Small plants catch the eye because they seem to have been molded of clay. In time, they branch irregularly and become a treelike shrub. Shiny long green leaves are attractive, though not produced in any great abundance.

FLOWER DESCRIPTION:
Flowers are brilliant red to pink and appear in clusters at branch tips in summer. Funnel-shaped blooms are 2 inches or more in diameter.

PROPAGATION: Seed, sometimes cuttings.
CULTURE: Keep plant underpotted in loose soil. Provide ample water and fertilizer during the growing season. A minimum temperature of 65° F. is absolutely necessary the whole year-round. Takes many years to reach even 3 feet. A rather difficult plant to manage, and not recommended for a beginner.

RECOMMENDED SPECIES:
A. multiflorum. Not a recognized species but listed under this name. Available: 7, 9, 22, 33.

A. obesum (desert rose). Shrub or small tree to 15 feet. Pink flowers. Available: 16, 25, 31, 33.

Aeonium tabuliforme

Adromischus species   Aeonium haworthii

Adromischus
(ah-dro-*miss*-kus)

FAMILY: Crassulaceae
ORIGIN: Central to southern Africa

GENERAL DESCRIPTION:
These stout-stalked succulent herbs or small bushes have a wide variety of interesting leaves, which sometimes form rosettes. Foliar color can range from green to grayish-blue, sometimes marked with splotches of maroon or purple. Many leaves are smooth; other species have a crinkled texture, caused by small warts on the leaves' skin, that is not unlike a raisin. Aerial roots are sometimes produced along the stems. When dry, they resemble Spanish moss.

FLOWER DESCRIPTION:
Small whitish or reddish flowers are borne on short spikes from the top of the plant in summer. They are unattractive and insignificant.

PROPAGATION: Stem and leaf cuttings.
CULTURE: General succulent culture. Water very lightly during winter dormancy. Plants should be exposed to sun to bring out best coloration. They do well indoors and under lights. Their short, gnarled trunks make them beautiful bonsai specimens.

RECOMMENDED SPECIES:
A. cooperii (plover-eggs). Light green leaves with purplish-red flowers. Available: 15, 17, 22, 24.
A. cristatus (crinkle-leaf plant). Stems covered with many red-brown aerial roots. Widely available.
A. festivus. Purplish-brown spotted leaves. Widely available.
A. maculatus (calico-hearts). Brown-spotted leaves. Available: 15, 17, 18, 22, 24, 33.

Aeonium
(ay-*oh*-nee-um)

FAMILY: Crassulaceae
ORIGIN: Mediterranean islands, western part of North Africa

GENERAL DESCRIPTION:
Variety is the word for aeoniums. Some grow into large bushes; others make just one large rosette to 16 inches. Leaves are glossy and range from apple-green to a very dark maroon tinged red.

FLOWER DESCRIPTION:
Flowers are usually yellow. They make up for their small size by the profusion produced at the ends of long stems. The blooming season varies greatly among the various species. Each stem flowers over a long period while other flowers come and go. They can be cut and used in arrangements, but stems of leaves are more dramatic.

PROPAGATION: Seed, cuttings.
CULTURE: Very easy to grow. Although aeoniums are succulent, they need more than average water and food to grow their best. Without sufficient water they just stand still and, if neglected enough, just seem to shrivel away. Full sun or partial shade suits them. Aeoniums make good land-scape plants in frost-free areas. Potted specimens require large containers.

RECOMMENDED SPECIES:
A. arboreum. Can become a large, spreading bush with multiple branches. Glossy green rosettes. Bright yellow flowers. Leaf stems cut well and last for two to three weeks. Leaves fall from the back of the rosette after turning brown and curling. Flowers winter-spring. Widely available.

A. arboreum 'atropurpureum.' Rosettes are dark maroon. A good accent among predominantly green plants. Widely available.
A. haworthii (pinwheel plant). Rounded shrub of red-edged blue-green rosettes. Flowers in spring. Widely available.
A. lindleyi. Small shrub to only 1 foot. Yellow flowers in summer. Available: 6, 7, 22, 31, 33, 36.
A. x 'schwarzkopf' Black rosettes. Unusual addition to any planting. Available: 6, 7, 15, 18, 22, 31, 36.
A. tabuliforme. Low-growing, flat, green rosettes up to 12 inches in diameter. Yellow flowers in summer. Available: 6, 13, 16, 22, 35, 36.

Aloe nobilis

Agave victoriae-reginae

Agave species

Agave
(ah-*gah*-vay)

FAMILY: Agavaceae
ORIGIN: North and South America

GENERAL DESCRIPTION:
Members of this large genus grow in rosette forms, ranging from mature sizes of 3 inches to 8 feet in diameter, depending upon the species. Stems are generally very short. The leaves of an agave are succulent, shaped like long triangles. They range in color from glaucous gray to dark green to pale apple-green, sometimes marked with white lines. Some species' leaves have hooked spines on their edges.

FLOWER DESCRIPTION:
White to yellow-green flowers are borne on long terminal stalks that come from the center of the rosette. These bear hundreds of small bell-to-tube-shaped flowers at one time. The agave flowers only once, after which its individual rosettes die. Flowering is dependent upon maturity. It is a signal that the plant has stored up enough energy to produce the stalk of flowers.

PROPAGATION: Offsets, bulbils, seeds.
CULTURE: General succulent culture. The agave is very easy to grow, a good beginner's plant. Generally speaking, it requires a large pot and plenty of water and fertilizer during its active growing season. In frost-free areas, the large species make dramatic accents outdoors. They need little attention, but spread to take up considerable space. Generous cultural practices speed maturity and flowering.

RECOMMENDED SPECIES:
A. americana (century plant). Gray-green rosette to 8 feet in diameter. Available: 3, 6, 13, 16, 21, 23, 33.
A. attenuata. Green to gray-green, spineless, matures to landscape size. Available: 6, 13, 21, 31.
A. bracteosa. Pale or gray-green rosette has tiny marginal teeth, grows to 4 feet in diameter. Available: 6, 9, 13, 16.
A. parviflora. Dark green leaves with white lines on upper surfaces, matures to only 6 inches in diameter. Available: 6, 7, 15, 22, 23, 25, 36.
A. utahensis 'nevadensis.' Glaucous green rosette that grows to a maximum of 16 inches. Available: 7, 13, 16.
A. victoriae-reginae. Very attractive. Dark green leaves with white lines on underside, grows to 12 inches. Widely available.

Aloe
(*al*-lo)

FAMILY: Liliaceae
ORIGIN: Drier regions of Africa, Madagascar

GENERAL DESCRIPTION:
There is a great diversity among the plants of this family. In overall form, they range from almost stemless plants to others that are 30 feet high. Some are rosettes of lance-shaped leaves; others are climbers, their long stems covered with dead leaves surmounted by rosettes. Leaf color varies from gray to all shades of green and glaucous blue. Spines are usually on the edges of the leaves. The spines of some species are sharp; those of others are short and soft. A few are spineless.

FLOWER DESCRIPTION:
Tubular flowers measure 1" to 1¼" long and are carried on stems above the foliage. Colors can be white-greenish to yellow, but shades of red and orange predominate among some of the commonly cultivated species. The bloom season varies considerably but is heaviest in autumn. Many species flower periodically all year.

PROPAGATION: Seed, offsets.
CULTURE: General succulent culture. On the whole, aloes are easy to grow in containers or in the ground where weather permits. Some of the very small species are difficult to manage. In general, the main key to successful culture is well-drained soil and lots of water. Some take full sun; others must have shade or filtered light. Be sure to check light requirements wherever you buy the plants.

Continued on next page

Anacampseros species

Aloe plicatilis

Aporocactus
flagelliformis

Aloe, continued

Species well suited to containers include: *A. aristata, A. barbadensis* (commonly sold as *A. vera*), *A. humilis, A. plicatilis, A. rauhii, A. variegata.*

RECOMMENDED SPECIES:
A. aristata. (torch plant, lace aloe). Stemless rosettes edged with soft white teeth. Widely available.

A. barbadensis (green aloe, burn aloe, *A. vera*). Stemless plant with green leaves. Juice of leaves effective for minor burns. Widely available.

A. brevifolia. Stemless rosettes of glaucous green leaves armed with sharp white teeth. Widely available.

A distans (jewelled aloe). Dense clumps of glaucous green leaves edged with yellow teeth. Flowers borne on long creeping stems. Available: 13, 16, 20, 22, 24, 33.

A. ferox (Cape aloe). Long lance-shaped leaves, green tinged red, on tall stems. Available: 13, 16, 20, 23, 24, 33.

A. humilis (spider aloe). Stemless clumps of glaucous green leaves edged with white teeth. Available: 6, 18, 23, 25.

A. nobilis (golden-tooth aloe). Lance-shaped green leaves edged with yellow teeth. Available: 3, 13, 15, 20, 21, 23, 26.

A. plicatilis. Large, glaucous green, toothed leaves on large shrub. Available: 6, 13, 23, 35, 36.

A. variegata (tiger aloe). White-spotted boat-shaped green leaves. Stemless. Widely available.

A. vera. (See *A. barbadensis*).

Anacampseros
(an-nah-*camp*-sair-ose)

FAMILY: Portulacaceae
ORIGIN: South Africa

GENERAL DESCRIPTION:
Small plants (usually under 6 inches when mature) form rosettes of leaves that are lance-shaped or almost round. Many are dark green, but there are other colors. The easiest ones to grow have hairy stems. The difficult ones are covered with scales that suggest bird droppings.

FLOWER DESCRIPTION:
Pink to light purple flowers are flat and wheel-shaped. They appear on and off during the year, but mostly in summer. They open in mid-afternoon, close in early evening.

PROPAGATION: Seed or cuttings.
CULTURE: General succulent culture. Hairy-stemmed plants are easy to grow. Keep them lightly shaded. Although they do not go completely dormant in winter, growth slows and they need less water. Species covered with papery scales are not recommended for beginners.

RECOMMENDED SPECIES:
A. lanceolata. Reddish flowers. Very long hairs on stems and leaves. Available: 15, 17, 20.

A. rufescens. Reddish-purple rosettes. Pink flowers. Available: 6, 13, 16, 20, 21, 22, 24.

Aporocactus
(ah-*pour*-o-kak-tus)

FAMILY: Cactaceae
GROUP: Hylocereus
ORIGIN: Southern Mexico, Central America

GENERAL DESCRIPTION:
Numerous pale-green, snakelike stems ½ inch in diameter, to 6 feet long. Each stem has 5 to 14 ribs. Many small bristly spines are a shade of pink when new, fading to horn-brown as they mature. Plant has aerial roots for gripping trees in its native habitat.

FLOWER DESCRIPTION:
Flowers are pink to red, funnelform, borne the length of the stem through spring, summer and fall. They measure from 2½ to 3 inches in length. They are very attractive.

PROPAGATION: Stem cuttings, occasionally grafts of stems onto upright cactus.
CULTURE: This epiphyte is best suited to hanging basket culture. Requires rich soil, filtered sun. Cannot tolerate frost.

RECOMMENDED SPECIES:
A. flagelliformis (rattail cactus). Crimson-pink flowers on long, slender stems. Available: 1, 13, 16, 21, 22, 27, 29, 31.

Ariocarpus retusus

Astrophytum
myriostigma

Aztekium ritteri

Ariocarpus
(air-ree-oh-*car*-pus)

FAMILY: Cactaceae
GROUP: Echinocactus
ORIGIN: Mexico, Texas

GENERAL DESCRIPTION:
Olive-brown to chalky-gray plants
are round with flattened top, 6 to 10
inches in diameter. The triangular
tubercles are almost leaflike. There
are no spines except for a few
occasional bristles at the tubercle tips.

FLOWER DESCRIPTION:
Pink, purple, or yellow flowers vary
in size, from 1¼" up to 3", and appear
in the center of the plant in autumn.
Some are urn-shaped, others wheel-
shaped.

PROPAGATION: Seed, but it takes
7 to 10 years for plant to look like
an ariocarpus.
CULTURE: General cactus culture.
Be sure to underpot, leaving only ½"
of room between the plant and
container. Water freely from April to
the end of September; taper off on
watering in the winter.

RECOMMENDED SPECIES:
A. fissuratus. Brownish-green
tubercles with light magenta flowers.
Available: 2, 8, 13, 15, 16, 22.

A. kotschoubeyanus. Dark olive-
green tubercles. White, rose, or light
purple flowers. The easiest to flower.
Available: 2, 7, 9, 13, 15, 16.

A. retusus (seven-stars). Gray or
blue-green tubercles; white flowers.
Available: 9, 13, 15, 16.

A. trigonus. Dark green tubercles;
yellow or cream-colored flowers. The
largest of the genus. Available: 9,
13, 15, 16.

Astrophytum
(as-tro-*fie*-tum)

FAMILY: Cactaceae
GROUP: Echinocactus
ORIGIN: Mexico

GENERAL DESCRIPTION:
All-green globular to cylindrical plants
have 4 to 10 ribs, grow to 6 inches
to 3 feet in height. All except
A ornatum and *A. capricorne* are
spineless. Several species are
covered with small tufts of hair.

FLOWER DESCRIPTION:
All species have yellowish flowers,
1" to 4" across. They are funnelform
or wheel-shaped and appear on the
top of the plant.

PROPAGATION: Seed. Seed-grown
plants are easier to cultivate than
those collected in the wild.
CULTURE: General cactus culture.

RECOMMENDED SPECIES:
A. asterias (sea urchin cactus).
Dome-shaped, with 8 deeply grooved
ribs. Spineless. Available: 2, 7, 8,
9, 13, 15, 22.

A. capricorne 'Aureum'. Very sharp
yellow spines. To 10" high.
Available: 7, 9, 25, 31.

A. myriostigma (bishop's-cap). White,
starlike scales dot grayish body.
Most have 5 ribs. Spineless.
Available: 5, 7, 8, 9, 13, 15.

A. myriostigma 'Nudum.' Dark green,
ribbed body without dotted surface
of *A. myriostigma*. Available: 7,
13, 15, 16, 22.

A. ornatum (star cactus). Cylindrical
shape to 14". Yellow spines, becoming
brown with age. Available: 7, 8,
13, 15, 16, 22.

Aztekium
(az-*tek*-ee-um)

FAMILY: Cactaceae
GROUP: Echinocactus
ORIGIN: Mexico

GENERAL DESCRIPTION:
Monotypic (a genus with only one
species). Globe-shaped gray-green
to green plant remains very small,
forming clusters as it matures. It has
alternating main and secondary ribs.
The main ribs have areoles; the
secondary ones do not. Very small
bristles form on new areoles at the top
of the plant but soon fall off.

FLOWER DESCRIPTION:
Minature half-inch funnelform flowers
are white to pink. They appear on
top of the plant off and on all spring
and summer.

PROPAGATION: Seed (a very slow
method) or grafting of offsets.
CULTURE: General cactus culture.
Essential to keep underpotted.
Aztekium is difficult to grow and not
recommended for beginners.

RECOMMENDED SPECIES:
A. ritteri. Clusters freely, forming mats,
but only after attaining maximum
growth. Adapts well to windowsill
culture. Available: 7, 9, 16, 20, 22, 24,
25, 31.

Borzicactus celsianus

Beaucarnea recurvata

Bowiea volubilis

Beaucarnea
(bo-*car*-nay-ah)

FAMILY: Agavaceae
ORIGIN: Mexico

GENERAL DESCRIPTION:
Beaucarnea eventually grows into a tree 20 feet tall. The trunk is gray-brown and, with age, covered with bark. The swollen base gives an over-all bottle appearance when young. This changes when plants age and begin to cluster. Long, thin, green leaves arch out all around the apex of the stem, creating a fountainlike effect.

FLOWER DESCRIPTION:
Insignificant flowers are beige and are borne in summer on a long stalk that rises from the top of the plant only after it is several years old.

PROPAGATION: Purchased seed. The sexes are on separate plants so chances of harvesting one's own seed are remote.
CULTURE: Given plenty of water, food, humus in the soil and bright light beaucarneas are fast growers. They make ideal houseplants, grow well in seemingly small pots and need repotting only every three or four years. Due to their arching foliage, they require a fair amount of growing room.

RECOMMENDED SPECIES:
B. recurvata (elephant-foot tree, ponytail). Very long, rather sharp-edged, thin, curving green leaves. Available: 6, 7, 15, 16, 22, 25, 31.
B. stricta. Straight glaucous green leaves have yellow margins. Available: 6, 7, 20, 22, 25.

Borzicactus
(*bohr*-zee-*kak*-tus)

FAMILY: Cactaceae
GROUP: Cereus
ORIGIN: Ecuador, Chile, Bolivia, Peru.

GENERAL DESCRIPTION:
The medium to dark waxy green borzicactus can grow to a height of 3 feet. The upright columns have distinct ribs and sharp, honey-colored spines. A few species have soft, hairy spines.

FLOWER DESCRIPTION:
The red tubular or funnelform flowers are usually irregularly shaped. They measure from 2″ to 3″ long and are produced near the top of the plant in the summer.

PROPAGATION: Seed and cuttings.
CULTURE: General cactus culture. A very robust plant, if somewhat slow grower.

RECOMMENDED SPECIES:
B. celsianus (Oreocereus celsianus), (Old-man-of-the-mountains, South American old-man). Matted hairs with yellow to red spines. Tubular red flowers. Available: 5, 7, 13, 15, 16, 20, 22.
B. trollii (Oreocereus trollii) (Old-man-of-the-Andes). Hairy with light yellow to reddish spines. Rose-colored flowers. Available: 13, 15, 16, 18, 20, 22.

Bowiea
(*bow*-ee-ya)

FAMILY: Liliaceae
ORIGIN: South Africa, tropical East Africa

GENERAL DESCRIPTION:
This curiosity of the plant world grows from a light green bulb that rests on the surface of the soil. A bulb measures 6 inches across at maturity and forms large clusters. Pale green branching stems emerge from the top of the bulb and need staking. If not supported, they will climb on anything nearby. Stems are thin and lacy but when several grow from the same bulb they form a great spidery web.

FLOWER DESCRIPTION:
One-inch greenish-white flowers are produced all along the stems in great profusion from spring to fall.

PROPAGATION: Offsets or bulb scale.
CULTURE: Provide ample water and well-drained soil. Feed regularly during the growing season. Stop watering and feeding when stems start to yellow and the plant goes dormant — usually in winter. Bowiea is an excellent houseplant, and it will thrive outdoors in the ground where there is no hard frost.

RECOMMENDED SPECIES:
B. volubilis (climbing onion). The only bowiea currently listed in catalogs. Available: 6, 7, 31.

Caralluma nebrownii

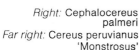
Right: Cephalocereus
palmeri
Far right: Cereus peruvianus
'Monstrosus'

Caralluma
(care-ah-*loo*-mah)

FAMILY: Asclepiadaceae
ORIGIN: North Africa to Asia, to
South Africa.

GENERAL DESCRIPTION:
Clumps of leafless, finger-shaped
stems range from purple-gray to
green, with great variation according
to species. The jointed stems, with
small teeth at the angles, measure
from 2" to 12" long depending
upon the species.

FLOWER DESCRIPTION:
Carallumas are grown for their
brightly colored, showy flowers. They
are shaped like 5-pointed stars, with
colors that include cream-white,
many shades of yellow, and dramatic
purples and deep reds. They can be
from ½" to 4" across, depending on
species. Flowers appear on the stems
in spring, summer and fall. While
their carion scent is strong and
unpleasant, many collectors find
they can overlook.the inconvenience
in exchange for the caralluma's
stunning flowers.

PROPAGATION: Seed, cuttings.
CULTURE: General stapeliad culture.
Carallumas range from being easy-to-
grow to very difficult, varying with
different species.

RECOMMENDED SPECIES:
C. europea. Easy to grow. Yellow
flowers with purple stripes and tips.
Available: 7, 13, 31, 36.
C. nebrownii. Clusters of deep red-
brown to blackish-brown flowers.
Easy to grow. Available: 5, 16, 29,
33, 36.

Cephalocereus
(*sef*-ah-lo-*seer*-ee-us)

FAMILY: Cactaceae
GROUP: Cereus
ORIGIN: Mexico, South America

GENERAL DESCRIPTION:
The upright, cylindrical cephalocereus can reach a height of 10 feet,
with an 8" to 10" diameter. The
gray-green body is ribbed and has
long, sharp spines. The soft hairy
spines for which the genus is best
known develop either before maturity or after the formation of a
cephalium at the top of the plant.

FLOWER DESCRIPTION:
The relatively small white to red,
short, funnelform flowers are borne
on the top of the hairy cephalium.
Cephalocereus does not bloom until
the plant is at least 15 to 20 years old.
The flowers are nocturnal:

PROPAGATION: Seed, cuttings.
CULTURE: General cactus culture.
Easy to care for, but slow-growing.
A good windowsill specimen when
young.

RECOMMENDED SPECIES:
C. alensis. Long, slender stems
branching from base. Brownish
needle-shaped spines. Cephalium
has white or yellow hairs. Purplish
flowers. Available: 13, 16, 20, 24, 29.
C. palmeri (bald old-man). Thick
bluish-green ribbed stems topped
with dense white wool, and with
purplish to brownish flowers.
Available: 9, 13, 15, 16, 18, 22.
C. senilis (old-man cactus). Very
popular. Wooly body while still
immature. Rose-colored flowers.
Widely available.

Cereus
(*seer*-ee-us)

FAMILY: Cactaceae
GROUP: Cereus
ORIGIN: Southeastern Brazil to
northern Argentina

GENERAL DESCRIPTION:
The ribbed, cylindrical, many-
branching cereus can grow to a
towering 15- or 20-foot height. The
slender stems are blue-green to gray-
green and have straight, needle-
shaped radial spines.

FLOWER DESCRIPTION:
Large, funnelform (6" to 8") white to
pink flowers are produced all along
the stems. They open at night during
the summer.

PROPAGATION: Seeds and cuttings.
CULTURE: General cactus culture.
This genus is the easiest of all cacti.
With generous culture, it is also the
fastest grower. Size can be restricted
by confining plant to small pot.

RECOMMENDED SPECIES:
C. peruvianus (Peruvian apple).
Shrubby or treelike growth habit
Green to gray-green with 6 to 8 ribs.
Available: 5, 9, 13, 15, 16, 22.
C. peruvianus 'Monstrosus' (giant-
club, curiosity plant). Approximately
12 ribs divided into irregular tubercles.
Spineless. Available: 5, 9, 13, 15, 16.

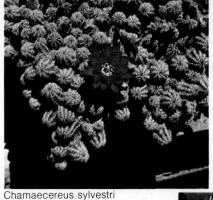

Chamaecereus sylvestri

Cissus juttae

Ceropegia woodii

Cissus tuberosa

Ceropegia
(sair-o-*peej*-yah)

FAMILY: Asclepiadaceae
ORIGIN: All of northeast, central and south Africa.

GENERAL DESCRIPTION:
The climbing or hanging stems of ceropegias have green leaves, some with silvery markings. As a general rule the leaves are small and quite succulent and come in widely varied and interesting shapes.

FLOWER DESCRIPTION:
The small flowers that appear all along the vines have succulent, bulbous bases and black petals that are joined at the tips. The majority of these unusual blossoms appear in summer, but many are also found in spring and fall.

PROPAGATION: Cuttings, tubers, seeds.
CULTURE: General succulent culture, except that ceropegias need more water. They make excellent hanging basket subjects, attractive and different house plants.

RECOMMENDED SPECIES:
C. cimiciodora. Very similar to *C. stapeliiformis.* Available: 7, 16, 31.
C. stapeliiformis. Thickly succulent stems. Flowers white with purple markings. Widely available.
C. woodii (rosary vine). Dark green leaves marbled with white. Widely available.

Chamaecereus
(kam-ee-*seer*-yus)

FAMILY: Cactaceae
GROUP: Echinocereus
ORIGIN: Western Argentina

GENERAL DESCRIPTION:
This popular monotypic genus has short clustering green stems that grow to 6″ long, ½″ diameter. They are ribbed and covered with short, bristly spines.

FLOWER DESCRIPTION:
Chamaecereus has vivid red-scarlet flowers that appear in summer all along the stems. They are a long funnelform shape, measuring approximately 3 inches.

PROPAGATION: Cuttings.
CULTURE: General cactus culture. Very easy, a good beginner's plant. Does best in a shallow pot.

RECOMMENDED SPECIES:
C. sylvestri (peanut cactus). Widely available.
Many hybrids of *C. sylvestri* are also available. Worth watching the catalogs for.

Cissus
(*siss*-uhs)

FAMILY: Vitaceae
ORIGIN: South West Africa, Tanzania, Kenya

GENERAL DESCRIPTION:
Members of this grape family found most interesting by succulent collectors include species that have large, bulb-shaped, succulent, tuberous bases that sprout vines of green leaves. The caudexes can range to a maximum height of 10 feet, though those found in succulent collections are generally container-sized. The large jagged-edged triangular leaves and stems are deciduous.

FLOWER DESCRIPTION:
Small yellowish-green flowers are borne in clusters along the stems in the summer. Many species develop attractive, bright red fruit.

PROPAGATION: Cuttings, seed.
CULTURE: General succulent culture. Winter watering must be kept to a minimum.

RECOMMENDED SPECIES:
C. bainesii (African tree grape). Yellowish-green trunk. Hairy saw-toothed-edged leaves. Available: 33.
C. juttae. Fleshy bottlelike trunk with large, serrated, waxy-green leaves. Available: 31, 33.
C. quadrangula. (*C.quadrangularis,* Veldt grape). Succulent green four-sided stems. Large waxy-green leaves. Available: 20, 22, 25, 31, 33, 35.
C. tuberosa. Globe-shaped brown tuber with green, grapelike leaves. Available: 22, 25.

Cleistocactus hylacanthus

Cochemiea setispina

Conophytum collection

Conophytum elishae

Cleistocactus
(*kly*-sto-*kak*-tus)

FAMILY: Cactaceae
GROUP: Cereus
ORIGIN: South America

GENERAL DESCRIPTION:
The cylindrical green, clustering stems of the cleistocactus grow to a mature size of approximately 3″ in diameter, 2 to 3 feet high. Occasionally they grow to 10 feet high or become procumbent. The plants have many ribs and spines that vary from white to brown, dense to sparse.

FLOWER DESCRIPTION:
Red, scarlet, or orange flowers are borne the length of the stems during the summer. They are tubular-shaped, measuring 3″ to 4″ long, ⅜″ diameter.

PROPAGATION: Offsets, cuttings, and seeds.
CULTURE: General cactus culture. Good container plants. Relatively easy to grow.

RECOMMENDED SPECIES:
C. baumannii (scarlet-bugler). Two- to three-inch-long scarlet flowers; yellow to brown spines.
Available: 9, 13, 15, 16.

C. hylacanthus. Slender erect stems covered with many white spines. Bright red flowers. Widely available.

C. strausii (silver-torch). Tall stems (to 6 feet) covered with white spines. Red flowers. Available: 13, 16, 20, 22, 28, 31.

Cochemiea
(ko-*kee*-mee-ah)

FAMILY: cactaceae
GROUP: coryphantha
ORIGIN: Baja California

GENERAL DESCRIPTION:
Green cylindrical plants, some species ranging to 6 feet long. Stems cluster as the plant matures; the oldest stems occasionally become procumbent. Tubercles are arranged in a spiral. Most species have hooked central spines; some have radial spines.

FLOWER DESCRIPTION:
Flowers are bright red, tubular or hooded shape, measuring approximately 2 inches long, ⅜ inch in diameter. Flowers are borne on the upper axils of the plant in spring and summer.

PROPAGATION: Seed, cuttings.
CULTURE: General cactus culture.

RECOMMENDED SPECIES:
C. Poselgeri. Trailing stems to 6 feet long. Brown spines.
Available: 13, 16, 20, 28, 31.

C. Setispina. To 2 feet high. Densely covered with brown-tipped white spines. Available: 13, 16, 20, 31.

Conophytum
(kohn-oh-*fy*-tum)

FAMILY: Aizoaceae
ORIGIN: South Africa

GENERAL DESCRIPTION:
Like many other members of the mesembryanthemum mimicry group, the conophytum grows in stemless, clumping leaf pairs. Their round, thickly succulent foliage ranges in color from blue-green and gray-green to yellow-green. The skin is often speckled and leaves usually have windows at the top. The division between the stems is a tiny slit at the top of the plant. Each year the outer shell of the old leaf pair dries and splits to expose 2 new leaves.

FLOWER DESCRIPTION:
The white to yellow dandelion-shaped flowers appear from the slit between the leaf pair, usually during our winter.

PROPAGATION: Seed, cuttings.
CULTURE: General mesembryanthemum culture. Due to winter blooming, summer watering must be minimal. Not recommended for beginners.

RECOMMENDED SPECIES:
C. elishae. Bluish-green leaves dotted with darker green. Bright yellow flowers. Available: 22, 24, 31, 34.

C. nevillei. Pale green leaves, gray-green spots. Available: 15, 22, 24, 31.

Copiapoa species

Coryphantha cornifera

Cotyledon undulata

Cotyledon
ladysmithiensis

Copiapoa
(*ko*-pee-ah-*po*-ah)

FAMILY: Cactaceae
GROUP: Echinocactus
ORIGIN: Chile

GENERAL DESCRIPTION:
Globe-shaped to oblong stems grow as clumps or solitary stems; all have ribs. The genus is characterized by radial spines and stems that are topped with woolly growth.

FLOWER DESCRIPTION:
Yellow bell-shaped to funnelform flowers appear at the plant's woolly apex in the spring and summer. These blooms are approximately 1½" long.

PROPAGATION: Seed, cuttings.
CULTURE: General cactus culture.

RECOMMENDED SPECIES:
C. humilis. Available: 5, 8, 13, 16, 31.
C. tennuisima 'cristata'. Available: 5, 8, 13, 15, 16.

Coryphantha
(kohr-ee-*fan*-thuh)

FAMILY: Cactaceae
GROUP: Coryphantha
ORIGIN: Mexico, Cuba, southern U.S.

GENERAL DESCRIPTION:
Green to gray-green stems are globular to cylindrical, solitary or clustering. All species have tubercles, some fat, others very narrow and pronounced. Spines are clustered at tubercle ends.

FLOWER DESCRIPTION:
The wide funnelform flowers are, generally speaking, large in relation to the plant. They open during the day, close at night during their bloom season, from spring to summer. Colors are widely varied according to species, ranging from greenish-yellow to white, through pink and violet.

PROPAGATION: Seed, cuttings.
CULTURE: General cactus culture.

RECOMMENDED SPECIES:
C. cornifera. Solitary globular stems with yellowish spines, yellow flowers. Available: 13, 15, 16, 24, 28.
C. macromeris. Clustering stems with white needle-shaped spines, purple flowers. Available: 2, 9, 15, 18, 20, 22, 24.
C. macromeris 'Runyonii'. Gray-green stems with pronounced tubercles. Purple flowers. Available: 9, 13, 15, 16.
C. runyonii. See: *C. macromeris* 'Runyonii'.

Cotyledon
(*koh*-till-*ee*-duhn)

FAMILY: Crassulaceae
ORIGIN: South Africa to Arabia

GENERAL DESCRIPTION:
Cotyledons represent a large and diverse genus. They can best be characterized as shrubby succulent plants whose mature sizes range from a few inches to several feet. Most species grown by collectors have persistent, succulent leaves in colors ranging from yellow-green to blue-gray.

FLOWER DESCRIPTION:
Bell-shaped, yellow to red flowers are pendant on long stalks borne above the leaves during spring and summer.

PROPAGATION: Cuttings, seed.
CULTURE: General succulent culture. Many cotyledons need exposure to bright light to bring out maximum foliar color.

RECOMMENDED SPECIES:
C. ladysmithiensis. Small shrub with hairy pale green leaves, tipped with brown. Widely available.
C. orbiculata. Red-margined leaves. Red flowers on long stalks. Available: 13, 16, 18, 20, 31, 33, 36.
C. paniculata (botterboom). Large shrub with papery-barked trunk. Deciduous leaves. Available: 6, 16, 22, 25, 33, 36.
C. undulata (silver-crown). Large, succulent wavy-edged leaves. Available: 6, 13, 16, 18, 22, 24, 33.

Crassula species

Crassula species

Crassula argentea
'Variegata'

Dasylirion 'Wheeleri'

Cycas revoluta

Crassula
(*krass*-yuh-lah)

FAMILY: Crassulaceae
ORIGIN: Southeastern Africa

GENERAL DESCRIPTION:
This large genus of succulent shrubs can be best described as a widely diversified plant group, characterized by unusual and varied leaf forms, arrangements and colors.

FLOWER DESCRIPTION:
Small white to red or yellowish flowers are borne in clusters on stems above the plants. Most crassulas bloom in spring and summer.

PROPAGATION: Stem and leaf cuttings, seed.
CULTURE: General succulent culture. Crassulas are very tender to frost.

RECOMMENDED SPECIES:
C. arborescens (silver jade plant). Glaucous gray leaves with red margins. Plant seldom flowers. Widely available.
C. argentea (jade tree, baby jade). Green leaves, white flowers. Very popular. Easy to grow. Widely available.
C. falcata (scarlet-paint-brush, airplane plant). Long sickle-shaped gray-green leaves. Cluster of scarlet flowers above foliage. Widely available.
C. lycopodioides (moss crassula, rattail crassula). Slender hanging or climbing stems with tiny green scale-like leaves. Widely available.
C. 'Morgan's Pink'. Fragrant salmon to rose-colored flowers, small clustering leaves. Widely available.
C. perforata (string-of-buttons). Widely available.
C. teres (rattlesnake). Narrow cylindrical plant composed of closely arranged, pale green leaves. Widely available.

Cycas
(*sy*-kuhs)

FAMILY: Cycadaceae
ORIGIN: Old World tropics

GENERAL DESCRIPTION:
These palmlike plants have thick, succulent trunks that are frequently covered with a shaggy brown bark. Many stiff, narrow green leaflets are borne on arching green stems in an opposite arrangement. Members of the closely related genera ceratozamia, dioon, enchephalartos and zamia share cycas' leaf arrangement, though foliar color, texture and shape is varied.

FLOWER DESCRIPTION:
Cycads bear cones at the top of their trunks. Female plants have larger cones. Plants of both sexes must bear cones simultaneously to produce viable seed.

PROPAGATION: Offsets, seed.
CULTURE: Easy but slow-growing plants are good landscape subjects in frost-free climates. They make ideal house plants and attractive bonsai specimens.

RECOMMENDED SPECIES:
C. revoluta (sago palm). A popular bonsai specimen. Available: 15, 25, 31, 32.

Dasylirion
(dah-zee-*leer*-yohn)

FAMILY: Agavaceae
ORIGIN: Southwestern U.S., Mexico

GENERAL DESCRIPTION:
The very long, slender, stemless leaves of dasylirion form a fountain-like rosette up to 6' diameter. The leaves usually have small teeth on their margins.

FLOWER DESCRIPTION:
Cream-white flowers are borne in clusters on a long stalk in spring and summer.

PROPAGATION: Seed.
CULTURE: General succulent culture.

RECOMMENDED SPECIES:
D. 'Wheeleri.' Yellow teeth edge green leaves. Widely available.

Dinteranthus puberulus

Dioscorea elephantipes

Diplocyatha ciliata

Dinteranthus
(din-tair-*an*-thus)

FAMILY: Aizoaceae
ORIGIN: South Africa

GENERAL DESCRIPTION:
Thickly succulent stemless whitish leaf pairs mimic surrounding stones in their native habitat. These small leaf pairs grow in clumps that rarely exceed 6" diameter.

FLOWER DESCRIPTION:
Yellow dandelionlike flowers appear in winter at the split between the leaf pair.

PROPAGATION: Seed.
CULTURE: General mesembryanthemum culture. A winter bloom cycle means that this plant needs water November through March; dry summers. Not recommended for beginners.

RECOMMENDED SPECIES:
D. puberulus (flowering-stone). Brownish gray-green skin with dark green dots. Available: 2, 5, 22, 36.

Dioscorea
(die-ose-*kore*-ee-ya)

FAMILY: Dioscoreaceae
ORIGIN: Mexico, South Africa

GENERAL DESCRIPTION:
The distinctive brown tuber of the dioscorea resembles a tortoise shell. It can range in size from 4 inches to 2 feet in diameter. A thin vine, that can be up to 30 feet long, emerges from the tuber. It has small, green, heart-shaped leaves. During the dioscorea's 3- to 4-month long dormancy, both leaves and vine are usually dropped.

FLOWER DESCRIPTION:
Clusters of small, starlike greenish-yellow flowers appear in late summer. they are insignificant. The dioscorea is cultivated more as a curiosity than as a foliage or flower plant.

PROPAGATION: Seed.
CULTURE: The cultural needs of the dioscorea are closer to those of house plants than of succulents. The plant should be placed in a container with about an inch of very porous soil above the outer edge of the tuber. The dioscorea should not be allowed to dry out completely between waterings.

RECOMMENDED SPECIES:
D. elephantipes. (Elephant's-foot). Tuber resembles tortoise shell. Twining stems. Available: 6, 9, 20, 25.
D. macrostachya. Available: 6, 9, 20, 31.

Diplocyatha
(dip-lo-sigh-*ath*-ah)

FAMILY: Asclepiadaceae
ORIGIN: South Africa

GENERAL DESCRIPTION:
The gray-green, leafless succulent stems of dipocyatha grow in small clusters, seldom exceeding 3" long. They have riblike angles that are armed with soft teeth.

FLOWER DESCRIPTION:
Like other stapeliads the dipocyatha has dramatic starfish-shaped flowers. The beige blooms are spotted with maroon, and appear from the base of the stems during the growing season. Flowers are rimmed with hanging tassles.

PROPAGATION: Cuttings.
CULTURE: General stapeliad culture. Diplocyatha is among the most easily cultivated stapeliads.

RECOMMENDED SPECIES:
D. Ciliata (Orbea ciliata). Available: 5, 7, 15.

Dudleya brittonii

Dolichothele species

Dyckia fosteriana

Dolichothele
(*dol*-ee-ko-*thee*-lee)

FAMILY: Cactaceae
GROUP: Coryphantha
ORIGIN: Mexico, southwestern U.S.,
South America

GENERAL DESCRIPTION:
The clustering globe-shaped stems
have green tubercles. Depending
upon the species, each head can
measure up to 5″ diameter. Clusters
of spines are found at the
tubercles' tips.

FLOWER DESCRIPTION:
Funnelform flowers, generally large
in relation to the plant, are borne
in the upper tubercle axils in spring
and summer. Flower's color is white
to yellow.

PROPAGATION: Seed, cuttings.
CULTURE: General cactus culture.

RECOMMENDED SPECIES:
D. sphaerica. Fat green tubercles with
radial spines. Available: 2, 9, 15, 18
20, 22, 24.

Dudleya
(*dud*-lee-yah)

FAMILY: Crassulaceae
ORIGIN: Washington to Baja California

GENERAL DESCRIPTION:
The succulent long-triangular or
spindle-shaped leaves of the dudleya
form rosettes borne on fleshy stems
that can grow quite long. The
largest species of the genus grows to
a maximum diameter of 1½ feet.
Smaller-growing species seldom
surpass 6″ to 8.″ The most distinctive
characteristic of the dudleya is the
light green foliage. Once the plant
has matured, a powdery white bloom
appears on the leaves, giving them
a luminous glow. Foliage should not
be touched after the bloom has
appeared.

FLOWER DESCRIPTION:
Small, star-shaped orange, yellow or
white flowers are borne in clusters
on an upright stalk. Flowering
generally occurs in early spring to
early summer.

PROPAGATION: Cuttings, seed.
CULTURE: General succulent culture,
except that plants tend to want more
water in winter and spring than in
summer and fall.

RECOMMENDED SPECIES:
D. brittonii. Solitary rosettes of
powdery white leaves to 1½ feet
across. Available: 6, 13, 16, 22, 31.
D. farinosa. Small rosettes. Pale
yellow flowers. Available: 13, 16,
22, 33.

Dyckia
(*dee*-kyuh)

FAMILY: Bromeliaceae
ORIGIN: Brazil, Paraguay, Argentina

GENERAL DESCRIPTION:
These stemless rosettes are made up
of green- to maroon-colored leaves.
The foliage is generally stiff, armed
with sharply pointed tips and spiny
margins. A silvery overlay on the
leaves give the plant an attractive
appearance.

FLOWER DESCRIPTION:
Yellow, orange or red flowers are
borne on tall, slender stalks. There
are many small blooms in each
cluster. Dyckias bloom in the spring.

PROPAGATION: Seed, division.
CULTURE: Dyckias are well-suited
to being grown as rock garden
specimens in frost-free climates.
They also make excellent container-
grown greenhouse specimens.

RECOMMENDED SPECIES:
D. fosteriana 4″ rosette of silvery
leaves become bronzed when grown
in full sun. Spiny leaf margins. Bright
gold flowers. Available: 32, 33.
D. marnier-lapostollei. A recent
discovery. Thick, short leaves have
soft, velvety hairs and spiny margins.
Available: 32, 33.
D. remotiflora. Silvery green leaves
taper to a needle-like point. Large
orange-red flowers. Available: 32, 33.

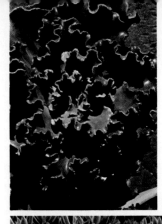
Echeveria
hybrid

Echinocactus grusonii

Echeveria
pulvinata

Echinocactus grusonii

Echeveria
(etch-a-*ver*-ya)

FAMILY: Crassulaceae
ORIGIN: Mexico to Venezuela

GENERAL DESCRIPTION:
All echeverias have in common a rosette form. Their greatly varied leaf color ranges from pale green through deep purple. Many are luminous pink. Generally speaking, the hairy-leaved species and hybrids are smaller growers, with narrow, not too succulent leaves. Many smooth-skinned species have very wide, thickly succulent leaves that form a large rosette (to 16 inches) resembling a head of leaf lettuce. Most echeverias are stemless or have very short stems.

FLOWER DESCRIPTION:
The long-lasting pendant flowers are red, pink or orange, borne on a stalk above the rosette. Each flower ranges in size from ¼" to 1" long, ¼" to ⅜" diameter. Blooming occurs in spring, summer, or fall, depending upon the species.

PROPAGATION: Cuttings of leaves, flower stalks, or offsets at base; occasionally from seed.

CULTURE: General succulent culture. Echeverias generally do well under generous cultural practices—more water, more fertilizer, and a richer soil than is required by many succulents. Exposure to light has direct effect upon intensity of foliar color. If stems become leggy, plant should be cut and rerooted.

RECOMMENDED SPECIES:
E. affinis. Bright green to greenish-black oblong leaves; red flowers. Widely available.

E. agavoides (molded wax). Green leaves tinged with dark red. Red flowers tipped with yellow. Widely available.

E. 'Black Prince'. A hybrid with deep maroon foliage. Available: 5, 15, 22, 31, 35, 36.

E. derenbergii (painted-lady). Many thickly succulent, small, pointed, glaucous blue leaves form a tight rosette. Widely available.

E. elegans (pearl echeveria, Mexican-gem). Tight rosette of small glacous green leaves. Rose flowers tipped with yellow. Widely available.

E. 'Morning Light'. A hybrid with beautiful luminous pink foliage. Available: 18, 22, 35.

E. pulvinata (plush plant, chenille plant). Narrow dark green leaves covered with many fine, short hairs. Edges of foliage tinged with red. Widely available.

In addition to the species and hybrids listed above, there are many other fascinating and beautiful members of this large genus, all worthwhile choices for any collector.

Echinocactus
(*eh*-kin-no-*kak*-tus)

FAMILY: Cactaceae
GROUP: Echinocactus
ORIGIN: Texas to Mexico

GENERAL DESCRIPTION:
Shiny, green, globe-shaped echinocacti are popular for their form and numerous sharp, brightly colored spines, which range from straw-yellow to shades of red. They can grow to a very large size, given the room, many topping a 3-foot diameter. When young, they have tubercles, which turn into ribs as the plants mature, generally by the time they are 15 years old.

FLOWER DESCRIPTION:
Two-inch-long pink to yellow bell-shaped flowers are borne on the top, wooly part of the echinocactus. The plant flowers in summer.

PROPAGATION: Seed.
CULTURE: General cactus culture. Relatively easy to grow, the echinocactus makes a good house plant, tolerant of low light indoors.

RECOMMENDED SPECIES:
E. grusonii. Widely available.

Echinopsis hybrid

Echinocereus
species

Edithcolea
grandis

Echinocereus
(eh-kin-o-*seer*-ee-us)

FAMILY: Cactaceae
GROUP: Echinocereus
ORIGIN: Southwest U.S. & Mexico

GENERAL DESCRIPTION:
Members of the genus echinocereus are generally upright cylindrical plants, measuring from 2" to 4" thick, and up to 2 feet high. Their green bodies have numerous ribs; spinal arrangement and color is widely varied among the species.

FLOWER DESCRIPTION:
Flowers, ranging from funnelform to bell-shaped, are predominantly metallic purple but a few species have yellow or pink blooms. The blossoms, usually measuring from 1" to 5", appear near the top of the plant in late spring or summer, often rupturing the skin of the cactus.

PROPAGATION: Seed and cuttings.
CULTURE: General cactus culture. Species native to Mexico are generally easier to grow than those native to the United States.

RECOMMENDED SPECIES:
E. cinerascens. White, needle-shaped spines. Rose to purple flowers. Available: 13, 15, 16, 18, 20, 28.

E. enneacanthus 'conglomeratus' (E. conglomeratus) (strawberry cactus). Many clustering stems densely covered with straw-colored spines. Purplish-red flowers. Not recommended for beginners. Available: 13, 16, 20, 28.

E. knippelianus. Solitary dark green stems, yellow spines, pink flowers. Not recommended for beginners. Widely available.

Echinopsis
(eh-kee-*nop*-sis)

FAMILY: Cactaceae
GROUP: Echinocereus
ORIGIN: South America

GENERAL DESCRIPTION:
Echinopsis is characterized by gray-green to green globular to oval stems that grow singly or in clusters. They are distinctly ribbed, occasionally with a few tubercles, and clusters of spines on areoles along the ribs.

FLOWER DESCRIPTION:
This genus is best known for its long-lasting, large, funnelform flowers. They range from white to pink, and are frequently up to 8 inches long.

PROPAGATION: Seed.
CULTURE: General cactus culture. Small-growing, free flowering species make good windowsill specimens.

RECOMMENDED SPECIES:
E. 'Haku-jo' A recently discovered sport, grown for its dark green body. Available: 5, 20, 22, 24, 31.

Because echinopsis has been extensively crossbred with lobivia and trichocereus, many nurseries list "E. hyb" and give description of flower color. These hybrids are often worth trying.

Edithcolea
(ee-dith-kole-ya)

FAMILY: Asclepiadaceae
ORIGIN: Socotra Island and Somalia

GENERAL DESCRIPTION:
The monotypic edithcolea has succulent beige and brown stems that sprawl and creep. They are angled and covered with small teeth. The plant is leafless.

FLOWER DESCRIPTION:
The edithcolea is grown for its beautiful flowers. They are very large (up to 4"), star-shaped, yellow with dark maroon markings. These flowers appear in summer.

PROPAGATION: Cuttings, seed.
CULTURE: This plant is very difficult to grow, recommended only for the most advanced collector. Its soil must be very porous, preferably high in pumice. Water frequently during the summer, not at all in winter.

RECOMMENDED SPECIES:
E. grandis.
Available: 9, 16, 31, 33.

Espostoa species

Epithelantha micromeris

Epiphyllum hybrids

Epiphyllum
(eh-pee-*fill*-uhm)

FAMILY: Cactaceae
GROUP: Hylocereus
ORIGIN: Central American tropics

GENERAL DESCRIPTION:
These tropical epiphytes have long green stems that hang or climb, reaching up to 200' in their native habitat. They are often cylindrical, the oldest growth becoming woody as it ages. Younger branches are flat or have 3 ribs. Some species are spineless, others have tiny, bristly spines clustered at intervals along the stem margins.

FLOWER DESCRIPTION:
Epiphyllums are grown for their large, showy blooms. Species blooms are white; the extensively hybridized varieties range through red, yellow, orange, and pink, many having intense coloration. They are borne the length of the stems, opening during the day or nocturnally, depending upon the species, in the spring and early summer.

PROPAGATION: Cuttings, seed.
CULTURE: General tropical cactus culture. Epiphyllums need a soil rich in humous and filtered sun. They are perfectly suited to hanging basket culture.

RECOMMENDED SPECIES:
E. chrysocardium. Available: 35.

Many beautiful hybrids (shown in the photos above) are available from specialist nurseries. Write for catalogs: 11, 14, 30.

Epithelantha
(eh-pee-thel-*an*-tha)

FAMILY: Cactaceae
GROUP: Echinocactus
ORIGIN: Texas to Mexico

GENERAL DESCRIPTION:
The globular to short, cylindrical clustering stems of epithelantha are usually white. They grow to a maximum height of 4". They have tubercles and many small white spines.

FLOWER DESCRIPTION:
Small white to pink flowers are borne on the top of the plant from spring through fall. The fruit formed by pollinated flowers is interesting — it sits up like tiny pink fingers around the top of the plant.

PROPAGATION: Seed, offsets.
CULTURE: General cactus culture. Epithelantha is somewhat fussy about light requirements. It likes a sunny spot but cannot tolerate full sun all day.

RECOMMENDED SPECIES:
E. micromeris (button cactus). Globular stems with depressed apex. Widely available.

Escobaria
(ess-ko-*bahr*-ya)

FAMILY: Cactaceae
GROUP: Coryphantha
ORIGIN: Texas to Mexico

GENERAL DESCRIPTION:
Escobaria, often considered a sub-genus of Coryphantha, is characterized by whitish cylindrical stems that grow to a maximum height of 8". The stems have fat to triangular tubercles and numerous short white spines with dark tips.

FLOWER DESCRIPTION:
White to pink small funnelform flowers appear at the top of the plant in spring and summer.

PROPAGATION: Seed, offsets.
CULTURE: General cactus culture. These plants need a very open soil mix and careful watering.

RECOMMENDED SPECIES:
E. dasyacantha. Dark-tipped bristle-like spines. Pink flowers. Available: 13, 16, 28, 31.

Euphorbia
grandicornis

Espostoa lanata

Euphorbia milii

Euphorbia
cactus &
E. obesa

Espostoa
(ess-pohs-*toe*-uh)

FAMILY: Cactaceae
GROUP: Cereus
ORIGIN: Peru, Brazil

GENERAL DESCRIPTION:
The columnar stems of espostoa
have many ribs. Generally speaking,
the branching stems are very tall and
slender, reaching to 18 feet in height.
Soft, hairy, white and stouter yellowish
spines are along the ribs.

FLOWER DESCRIPTION:
Nocturnal white flowers are borne on
a lateral cephalium, composed of
specialized, hairy areoles on one
side of the stem. Blossoms are funnelform, to 2″ long.

PROPAGATION: Seed.
CULTURE: General cactus culture.

RECOMMENDED SPECIES:
E. lanata (cotton-ball, Peruvian old-
man). Grows to 18! White wool with
yellow or brownish spines.
Widely available.
E. melanostele. Brown wool, long,
black spines. Widely available.

Euphorbia
(yoo-*for*-bee-ah)

FAMILY: Euphorbiaceae
ORIGIN: Africa

GENERAL DESCRIPTION:
The genus euphorbia is too diverse
to allow more than a few generalizations. All species have a toxic, milky
sap, many are succulent. Mature
sizes can range from a few inches
to many feet. The euphorbia's leaves
are generally insignificant and
deciduous. Many species have
spines, though unlike cacti, they do
not grow out of areoles. In some
instances the spines are actually
dried flower stalks.

FLOWER DESCRIPTION:
Euphorbia flowers are usually quite
small, often yellow or greenish-
yellow. The flower consists only of a
unisexual male stamen or female
pistil, generally clustered together
and surrounded by colorful bracts
(specialized leaves). Time of bloom
for euphorbias depends upon both
species and cultural conditions.

PROPAGATION: Easiest from cuttings.
Sap must be coagulated by immer-
sion in cold water or powdered
charcoal. Allow callous to form, then
place in soil. Grafting is possible
provided another euphorbia
(*E. mammillaris* or *E. cereiformis*) is
used as stock. Cuts must be
coagulated and cleaned before
grafting. Seed, when obtainable, is
another acceptable method.

CULTURE: General succulent culture.
As a rule, euphorbias require a slightly
richer soil than do most cacti. They
make good houseplants, unbothered
by low humidity. Euphorbias need
bright light; grow well under artificial
lights.

RECOMMENDED SPECIES:
E. flanaganii 'cristata'. Ribbed, spiny
green stems. Widely available.
E. grandicornis (cow's-horn).
Succulent, spiny, branching gray-
green stems. Widely available.
E. horrida (African milk barrel).
Many spiny, succulent ribs. Widely
available.
E. mammillaris hyb. (corkscrew).
Dwarf, clustering tubercled cylinders.
Widely available.
E. milii (*E. spendens*, crown-of-
thorns). Twining spiny stems with
green leaves, bright pink bracts.
Widely available.
E. obesa (living-baseball). Spineless
globe-shaped succulent with gray
and green markings. Very unusual.
Widely available.
E. pseudocactus. Spiny, columnar,
ribbed succulent. Widely available.
E. splendens. See: *E. milli*.
E. submammillaris 'Corn Cob'. As the
name implies, looks like a corn cob.
Widely available.

Faucaria tigrina

Ferocactus macrodiscus

Fenestraria rhopalophylla

Faucaria
(foe-*kahr*-yuh)

FAMILY: Aizoaceae
ORIGIN: South Africa

GENERAL DESCRIPTION:
Very short-stemmed, succulent, triangular-shaped leaves have small teeth along their margins. The leaves grow in small, low clumps, ranging in color from glaucous green to olive green, often with spotting on the skin.

FLOWER DESCRIPTION:
Typical of the mesembryanthemums, faucaria has dandelion-like yellow to white flowers that open in summer.

PROPAGATION: Seed.
CULTURE: General mesembryanthemum culture. A good plant for beginners.

RECOMMENDED SPECIES:
F. tigrina (tiger's-jaws). Gray-green skin with white dots. Yellow flowers. Widely available.
F. tuberculosa. Dark green leaves with white warts on upperside.
Available: 7, 9, 15, 22.

Fenestraria
(fen-ess-*trah*-ree-ah)

FAMILY: Aizoaceae
ORIGIN: South Africa

GENERAL DESCRIPTION:
The thickly succulent, dull green stemless leaves of fenestraria clump to form a 2" to 2½" rosette. They have windows at the tops of their stems. Like lithops and lapidarias, these are mesembryanthumum mimicry group.

FLOWER DESCRIPTION:
Daisy-shaped yellow or white flowers are borne on a short stem above the leaves. Blossoms are relatively large, measuring from 2" to 3" diameter. Plants flower in summer.

PROPAGATION: Seed.
CULTURE: General mesembryanthemum culture. Not recommended for beginners. Watering and light requirements are quite precise.

RECOMMENDED SPECIES:
F. rhopalophylla (window plant, baby-toes). Glaucous green leaves with white flowers. Available: 13, 15, 16.

Ferocactus
(*fair*-o-kak-tus)

FAMILY: Cactaceae
GROUP: Echinocactus
ORIGIN: Southwestern U.S., Mexico

GENERAL DESCRIPTION:
The globe-shaped to columnar ferocactus varies in color from blue-green to green, has approximately 10 to 20 ribs. Its highly interesting, widely varied spines range from yellow to red. Most of them are very sharp and strong. Some species develop wool upon flowering.

FLOWER DESCRIPTION:
The yellow to red-purple flowers are funnelform to tulip-shaped, measuring 2" to 3." They appear at the top of the plant in summer, only after the ferocactus has been growing from seed for several years.

PROPAGATION: Seed.
CULTURE: General cactus culture. A good container plant. Slow growing.

RECOMMENDED SPECIES:
F. echidne. Globe-shaped cactus with straight yellow spines, yellow flowers. Available: 2, 13, 16, 20, 24, 28.
F. glaucescens (blue barrel cactus). A very distinct glaucous green with pale yellow spines, yellow flowers. Available: 13, 15, 16, 20, 24, 28.
F. latispinus (devil's-tongue). Depressed globe-shaped plant with yellow radial spines, red central spines. Purple-colored flowers. Available: 2, 5, 9, 13, 15, 16, 22.

F. macrodiscus. Depressed globe shape with curved spines, pink flowers. Available: 13, 15, 16, 28, 31.
F. wislizenii (fishhook cactus). Columnar with white radial spines, red, brown, or gray hooked central spines. Orange-red to yellow flowers. Available: 2, 13, 15, 16.

Frailea species

Fouquieria splendens

Gasteria hybrid

Fouquieria
(fou-*kee*-air-ee-ya)

FAMILY: Fouquieriaceae
ORIGIN: Southwest U.S., Mexico

GENERAL DESCRIPTION:
These treelike shrubs have swollen bases, and mottled skin, generally tan with stripes or blotches of green. The numerous lateral branches have green leaves. A few species are quite spiny, others only moderately so. A mature specimen ranges from 10' to 12' tall.

FLOWER DESCRIPTION:
The genus has two basic flower types; one small, bell-shaped and creamy white, the other long 1" to 1½" tubular and reddish. They are borne in clusters on the stems. Bloom time is unpredictable.

PROPAGATION: Cuttings, seed.
CULTURE: General succulent culture. Fouquieria requires a slightly more generous ration of water than do many succulents. Species with tuberous roots make good bonsai subjects.

RECOMMENDED SPECIES:
F. columnaris (*Idria columnaris*) (boojum tree). Conical trunk with spreading branches.
Available: 7, 25, 33.
F. splendens (ocotillo, coach-whip). Shrub with tubular red flowers.
Available: 1, 7, 18, 20, 25.

Frailea
(*fray*-lyuh)

FAMILY: Cactaceae
GROUP: Echinocactus
ORIGIN: Argentina, Paraguay

GENERAL DESCRIPTION:
Small-growing cacti that are generally wider than they are high, fraileas grow in clusters reaching a maximum of 2'. Stems are ribbed, skin usually a shade of green, sometimes with purple markings. Spines range from numerous and bristlelike to sparse and much stouter.

FLOWER DESCRIPTION:
One rarely sees the yellow flowers of frailea. They open only under the hottest, brightest sun. When open, they are funnelform, approximately 1½" long. Flowers that remain closed are self-pollinating; those that open must be pollinated by hand.

PROPAGATION: Seed, cuttings.
CULTURE: General cactus culture.

RECOMMENDED SPECIES:
F. cataphracta. Crescent-shaped purple markings below areoles. Bristlelike yellowish spines.
Available: 13, 16, 20, 28, 31.
F. grahliana. Top-shaped stems with curved yellow spines.
Available: 13, 16, 20, 22, 24, 29, 31.
F. schilinzkyana. Depressed globular stems with black spines.
Available: 15, 16, 20, 21.

Gasteria
(gas-*ter*-yuh)

FAMILY: Liliaceae
ORIGIN: South Africa

GENERAL DESCRIPTION:
The stemless leaves of gasteria form rosettes as the plant matures. The foliage is succulent, generally green to dark green with darker spotted markings. Some species have cream-colored markings with pink-tinged margins. Leaves measure to 1½" wide, 18" long.

FLOWER DESCRIPTION:
Curving tubular flowers measure 1" to 2" long. The red-orange blooms are borne on a long, nodding stalk during the summer.

PROPAGATION: Cuttings, seed.
CULTURE: General succulent culture. Gasterias can be grown in relatively shady locations.

RECOMMENDED SPECIES:
G. armstrongii. White markings on spiral leaf rosettes. Available: 13, 16, 18.
G. caespitosa (pencil-leaf). Narrow leaves spotted with light green.
Available: 13, 16, 18, 21, 22, 25.

Graptopetalum paraguayense

Gymnocalycium
saglione

Hatiora
salicorniodes

Gymnocalycium
species

Graptopetalum
(*grap*-toe-pet-uh-lum)

FAMILY: Crassulaceae
ORIGIN: Southwest U.S., Mexico

GENERAL DESCRIPTION:
Lovely rosettes of thickly succulent
leaves are borne on long stems. The
leaves are a luminous white with
pink-purple tones. Mature rosettes
measure approximately 3″ diameter.

FLOWER DESCRIPTION:
Straw-colored flowers with maroon
markings are bell-shaped, usually
carried on a pendant stalk in the
summer.

PROPAGATION: Stem or leaf cutting.
CULTURE: General succulent culture.
Graptopetalum is very easy to grow,
a good beginner's plant. It is particularly well-suited to being grown
in a hanging basket.

RECOMMENDED SPECIES:
G. paraguayense (ghost plant,
mother-of-pearl plant). A lovely
plant, available in many retail garden
centers and plant shops, catalogs:
7, 15, 20, 22, 24, 33, 35.

Gymnocalycium
(jim-no-kal-*iss*-yuhm)

FAMILY: Cactaceae
GROUP: Echinocactus
ORIGIN: Argentina to Brazil

GENERAL DESCRIPTION:
The globular stems of gymnocalycium
grow in clusters or singly, each stem
measuring to 12″ thick, depending
upon species. The green to gray-
green cacti have tubercled ribs and
clusters of spines that are stout,
but relatively sparse.

FLOWER DESCRIPTION:
The white to pink flowers are borne
near the top of the plant in spring and
summer. The edges of their petals
are often green or purple. They are
bell-shaped to short funnelform,
measuring up to 3″ long.
PROPAGATION: Seed.
CULTURE: General cactus culture.

RECOMMENDED SPECIES:
G. baldianum. Dark gray-green stems.
Wine-red flowers. Available: 13, 15,
16, 18, 20, 24, 31.
G. denudatum (spider cactus).
Yellowish needle-shaped spines.
White to pale rose flowers.
Widely available.
G. saglione. Solitary stems to 12″
thick. White or pink flowers.
Available: 5, 8, 13, 15, 16.

Hamatocactus
See: Ferocactus.

Hatiora
(hah-tee-*or*-uh)

FAMILY: Cactaceae
GROUP: Rhipsalis
ORIGIN: Brazil

GENERAL DESCRIPTION:
The leafless jointed stems of hatiora
form small pendant bushes. They are
spineless; growing to a maximum of
18″ in diameter.

FLOWER DESCRIPTION:
A profusion of round, bright yellow
flowers with red markings are borne
in the axils of the stems during the
spring and summer.

PROPAGATION: Cuttings, sometimes
seed.
CULTURE: General tropical cactus
culture. This epiphyte requires a
humus-rich soil, filtered sun.

RECOMMENDED SPECIES:
H. salicornioides (spice cactus,
drunkard's dream). Available: 20, 22,
24, 28, 29, 31.

Above, top: Haworthia species
Above: Haworthia truncata

Hoya bella

Haworthia collection

Haworthia
(hah-*worth*-yuh)

FAMILY: Liliaceae
ORIGIN: South Africa

GENERAL DESCRIPTION:
Stemless leaves form rosettes ranging from 1″ to 6″. Many leaves are shaped like long, narrow triangles. They are primarily dark green with many color variations, including blue-green, red and brown. They are accented with white markings that are tiny warts. Species with shorter, more succulent, smooth-skinned leaves are more sun tolerant. They are generally a lighter green and have windows along their upper surfaces for filtering sunlight.

FLOWER DESCRIPTION:
The small, relatively insignificant flowers are borne in clusters on long stems from the center of the plant. Flowers are usually white with stripes of light green or pale pink in petal centers. Blossoming can be at any time of year, depending on species.

PROPAGATION: Division. Cuttings of slow-growing species occasionally done. Seed possible but unreliable.
CULTURE: General succulent culture. Haworthias can tolerate shady conditions, but need bright light (not full sun) to bring out maximum coloration and texture. Requirements vary with each species. Dormancy can occur in summer or winter, depending upon species, and can be accompanied by root loss. Plants with dead or dying roots should be cleaned and repotted in fresh soil. Narrow-leaved haworthias require more water than many succulents. Thickly succulent species and plants with large tap roots must be watered carefully year-round.

RECOMMENDED SPECIES:
H. attenuata. Long dark green leaves with white markings. Shade lover. Available: 13, 15, 16, 22, 31, 33.
H. cuspidata. Pale green thickly succulent leaves with windows. Widely available.
H. fasciata (zebra haworthia). Glossy green long triangular leaves with white markings. Widely available.
H. limifolia (fairy-washboard). Dark green-brown ribbed leaves. Widely available.
H. retusa. Pale green thickly succulent leaves with windows, pointed tips. Widely available.
H. tessellata. Succulent dark green triangular leaves with windows, pale green markings. Widely available.
H. truncata. Dark greenish-brown thickly succulent leaves with windows. Widely available.

Homalocephala
See: Echinocactus.

Hoya
(*hoy*-uh)

FAMILY: Asclepiadaceae
ORIGIN: China, India, Malayan archipelago, Australia.

GENERAL DESCRIPTION:
Hoyas grow as evergreen climbing or twining vines, or as loose shrubs. The succulent species have green waxy-looking leaves.

FLOWER DESCRIPTION:
Fragrant clusters of star-shaped flowers are borne along the stems in summer and fall. Colors are generally yellow to white with red, purple or brown markings. Blossoms should never be cut off, as they are the growing point for the next crop of flowers.

PROPAGATION: Cuttings.
CULTURE: General stapeliad culture. Hoyas prefer well-drained, moder — ately rich soil and filtered sun.

RECOMMENDED SPECIES:
H. bella (miniature wax plant). Many-branched dwarf shrub. Flowers white with deep crimson margins. An excellent hanging basket plant. Available: 20, 25, 29, 31.
H. carnosa (wax plant). Succulent shrub with trailing stems; flowers are white with red margins. Available: 7, 18, 20, 22, 29, 33, 37.

Hylocereus undatus

Huernia pillansii

Jatropha cathartica

Huernia
(*hwair*-nyuh)

FAMILY: Asclepiadaceae
ORIGIN: South Africa, East Africa, Arabia

GENERAL DESCRIPTION:
The soft, fleshy gray-green stems of huernia grow in large clumps and have prominent but soft teeth. Measuring approximately ½" across, 2" to 3" in length, they look somewhat like jointed fingers.

FLOWER DESCRIPTION:
Huernias are cultivated for their yellow, red-brown or dark maroon flowers. These star- to urn-shaped blooms measure from ⅜" to 3" across, generally appearing from the base of the stems in summer and early fall. They have a mild, but not offensive carion scent.

PROPAGATION: Cuttings, seed.
CULTURE: General stapeliad culture.

RECOMMENDED SPECIES:
H. hystrix. Crimson markings on yellow flowers. Available: 7, 9, 16, 33, 36.
H. pillansii (cocklebur). Stems densely covered with bristly teeth. Flowers yellow spotted with crimson. Available: 5, 13, 15, 16, 22, 24.

H. schneideriana (red dragon flower). Brownish-red flower with purple-black tubes. Available: 7, 13, 16, 22, 33.

Hylocereus
(hy-low-*seer*-yus)

FAMILY: Cactaceae
GROUP: Hylocereane
ORIGIN: Caribbean, Mexico, Central America

GENERAL DESCRIPTION:
The slender, 3-ribbed light green to yellow-green stems of the hylocereus climb or hang, in their native habitat sometimes reaching 200 feet in length. They have short, sparse spines.

FLOWER DESCRIPTION:
The hylocereus is grown mainly for its fragrant, very large white flowers. The funnelform blooms are to 12" long, 15" wide. Nocturnal bloomers, they open all along the stems in spring and summer.

PROPAGATION: Cuttings, seed.
CULTURE: General tropical cactus culture. Cannot stand heavy frost. Best suited to hanging basket culture.

RECOMMENDED SPECIES:
H. undatus (night-blooming cereus, queen-of-the-night). Beautiful white flowers. Available: 9, 18, 20, 21, 22, 31.

Jatropha
(juh-*tro*-fuh)

FAMILY: Euphorbiaceae
ORIGIN: Tropical regions of the world

GENERAL DESCRIPTION:
The caudex (bulbous rootstock) of the jatropha is gray. It has shrubby green foliage that is dropped when the plant goes dormant in winter.

FLOWER DESCRIPTION:
Small star-shaped red flowers are borne in clusters on annual stems in the summer.

PROPAGATION: Seed.
CULTURE: General succulent culture. Do not water during dormancy.

RECOMMENDED SPECIES:
J. berlandieri. See: *J. cathartica.*
J. cathartica (*J. berlandieri*). Slow-growing with spherical caudex. Available: 5, 7, 13, 15, 16, 22, 32.

Lapidaria margaretae

Lemaireocereus species

Kalanchoe
beharensis

Kalanchoe
(*kahl*-an-*ko*-ay)

FAMILY: Crassulaceae
ORIGIN: Tropical regions of the world, primarily Africa.

GENERAL DESCRIPTION:
Plants in this large genus are generally shrubby, ranging in size from a few inches to several feet. They are best noted for attractive, colorful leaves. They can be found in all shades of green, gray-green, blue-green, even bronzy browns and reds. Some leaves are variegated, some hairy, some smooth.

FLOWER DESCRIPTION:
The red, yellow, or white bell-shaped flowers of the kalanchoe are usually borne on stalks near the top of the plant during spring, summer, and fall.

PROPAGATION: Seed, cuttings and cuttings of plantlets formed in leaf notches.
CULTURE: General succulent culture. Relatively easy to grow. These plants will *not* tolerate frost.

RECOMMENDED SPECIES:
K. beharensis (feltbush, velvetleaf). Large, triangular scalloped leaves, covered with tiny hairs. Leaves are clustered at the tips of branches. Available: 13, 16, 20, 21, 24, 36.

K. blossfeldiana. Long-lasting blooms of scarlet, yellow and orange are borne in clusters above green foliage. Extensively hybridized. Widely available in retail nurseries and plant stores.

K. pumila. Small scallop-edged leaves. Rose to violet flowers. Widely available.

K. tomentosa (pussy-ears, panda plant). Gray-green leaves are covered with silvery hairs, tipped with brown. Very popular. Widely available.

Lapidaria
(lah-pi-*dahr*-yah)

FAMILY: Aizoaceae
ORIGIN: Southwest Africa

GENERAL DESCRIPTION:
This monotypic genus is another example of mesembryanthemum mimicry plants. The smooth-skinned, stemless pairs of leaves resemble very pale green stones. The thickly succulent leaves are approximately 1" long, ⅜" diameter.

FLOWER DESCRIPTION:
Daisylike flowers are yellow to cream-white, fading to pink as they age. The 1½" to 2" flowers appear in the summer.

PROPAGATION: Seed, sometimes offsets.
CULTURE: General mesembryanthemum culture. Not recommended for beginners.

RECOMMENDED SPECIES:
L. margaretae (Kangaroo rose). The only species of genus lapidaria. Available: 5, 15, 16, 22, 24, 31, 34.

Lemaireocereus
(lah-*mahr*-oh-seer-yus)

FAMILY: Cactaceae
GROUP: Cereus
ORIGIN: Mexico

GENERAL DESCRIPTION:
The ribbed, columnar lemaireocereus can grow to a height of 10 to 20 feet. It has a dull green skin and spines that vary from being extremely short to one inch or longer, and very stout.

FLOWER DESCRIPTION:
Lemaireocereus blooms only when it is very old. Its straw-colored to pale pinking bell-shaped flowers are small and relatively unattractive. They are borne along the sides on the ribs.

PROPAGATION: Seed, offsets.
CULTURE: General cactus culture. *Very* easy to grow. Though it will eventually outgrow a container, it can be a potted specimen for a long time.

RECOMMENDED SPECIES:
L. marginatus (organ-pipe cactus). Branching green cactus with needle-shaped spines. Available: 5, 9, 15, 20, 22, 26, 28.

L. pruinosis (powder-blue cereus). Thick glaucous-green stems, white to rose flowers. Available: 5, 14, 15, 20, 31.

L. thurberi (organ-pipe cactus). Brownish-black spines. Nocturnal white to purplish flowers. A very slow grower. Available: 5, 14, 15, 20, 31.

Leuchtenbergia principis

Lithops collection

Lobivia hybrid

Leuchtenbergia
(look-ten-*burg*-yah)

FAMILY: Cactaceae
GROUP: Echinocactus
ORIGIN: Mexico

GENERAL DESCRIPTION:
The columnar leuchtenbergia grows to a maximum height of 2 feet. Its triangular-shaped gray-green tubercles have purplish-red splotches at their tips. Old tubercles have a tendency to dry up and fall off, leaving the stalk exposed at the bottom. Leuchtenbergia has long, weak spines.

FLOWER DESCRIPTION:
Yellow funnelform to bell-shaped blooms appear at the tubercles' tips in the spring and summer, 3 to 4 years after its propagation by seed. They are approximately 4" long.

PROPAGATION: Seed.
CULTURE: General cactus culture.

RECOMMENDED SPECIES:
L. principis (agave cactus, prism cactus). The only known species of leuchtenbergia. Available: 9, 13, 15, 16, 22.

Lithops
(*lith*-ops)

FAMILY: Aizoaceae
ORIGIN: South Africa, Southwest Africa·

GENERAL DESCRIPTION:
Lithops are members of the mesembryanthemum mimicry group. Their short, very succulent leaves imitate both the shape and coloring of rocks. They grow in stemless clumps of paired leaves approximately 1" to 2" diameter.

FLOWER DESCRIPTION:
Yellow to white dandelion-shaped flowers emerge from between the leaves in November, December and January. The blooms are often as large as a pair of leaves.

PROPAGATION: Seed.
CULTURE: General membryanthemum culture. Because lithops are from the southern hemisphere, their summer is our winter. Watering during spring and summer months (March through September) must be very light. Increase watering in November. Lithops must be in very fast draining soil.

RECOMMENDED SPECIES:
L. bella. Brownish-yellow ochre coloring with green marbling, fragrant white flowers. Widely available.
L. lesliei. Gray-green skin; darker green windows marbled with rust-colored markings. Yellow-gold flowers have pale pink underside. Available: 10, 22, 31, 33, 34.
L. marmorata. Gray-green body with creamy-green mottlings in windows. White flowers. Available: 10, 22, 34.
L. verruculosa. Bluish-gray skin with dark red or gray warts. Orange-brown flowers. Available: 10, 22, 34.

Lobivia
(loh-*beev*-yuh)

FAMILY: Cactaceae
GROUP: Echinocereus
ORIGIN: Bolivia, Peru, Northern Argentina

GENERAL DESCRIPTION:
Generally small, globular cacti grow as single stems or clumping mats. The green stems have ribs, sometimes tubercled, and are covered with numerous weak spines.

FLOWER DESCRIPTION:
Lobivias are best known for their brilliantly colored yellow, red, and purple flowers. They flower freely and blooms are generally long lasting. The bell-shaped to short funnelform blossoms appear in spring and summer.

PROPAGATION: Seed, cuttings.
CULTURE: General cactus culture.

RECOMMENDED SPECIES:
L. binghamiana. Yellow spines, purplish-red flowers. Widely available.
L. caespitosa. Clumping stems with dark spines, orange flowers. Available: 13, 16, 20, 28, 29.
L. pentlandii. Solitary stems, brownish spines, rose-colored flowers. Available: 13, 20, 28, 29.

Mammillaria bocasana

Mamillopsis senilis

Mammillaria geminispina

Mammillaria
(mah-mih-*lahr*-yah)

FAMILY: Cactaceae
GROUP: Coryphantha
ORIGIN: Southwestern U.S., Mexico, Central America

GENERAL DESCRIPTION:
The numerous and wonderfully diverse members of genus mammillaria grow in globular to cylindrical shaped stems, often clumping, but sometimes remain solitary or become procumbent. Specimen sizes can range from tiny individual heads only a few inches wide to massive clumps. Tubercles are arranged in spiraling rows, distinguished from the closely related genus coryphantha by the lack of grooves in their tubercle tops and the location of flowers. The widely varied and distinctive spines come in all shapes, colors, sizes, textures and arrangements. They are largely responsible for the mammillaria's attractiveness.

FLOWER DESCRIPTION:
Small bell-shaped flowers come in many colors—white to cream, reds, pinks and yellows. Unlike other cacti, whose flowers are borne on areoles, mammillaria blooms arise from the joints of tubercles in a ring around the top of the plant. Blossoming occurs from March to October.

PROPAGATION: Easily grown from seed. Unrooted pups can be removed and potted up.
CULTURE: General cactus culture. Except for rebutias, mammillarias are the easiest cacti to grow and flower. Soil for very small species or plants with bag tap roots should be especially porous. Mammillarias require generous watering during spring and summer. They can withstand temperatures to near freezing if kept dry during the winter. Woolly varieties should be watered carefully to avoid damaging soft spines.

RECOMMENDED SPECIES:
M. albescens. Bristly yellowish spines. Greenish-white flowers. Available: 13, 15, 16, 20, 28, 31.
M. bocasana 'Inermis' (snowball cactus). Many hooked yellowish spines. Yellow flowers. Available: 5, 13, 16, 18, 20, 22, 28, 31.
M. columbiana. Solitary cylindrical stems. Deep pink flowers. Widely available.
M. collinisii. Widely available.
M. compressa. Woolly axils. Bristly white spines. Purplish-red flowers. Widely available.
M. elegans. Cylindrical stems with many needle-shaped white spines. Red flowers. Available: 5, 13, 15, 16, 22.
M. geminispina. Woolly white axils and soft white spines. Carmine flowers. Available: 5, 9, 13, 16, 22.
M. hemisphaerica. See *M. heyderi*.
M. heyderi (coral cactus). Brown-tipped white spines. Flowers white with red or pink. Available: 2, 13, 16, 18, 20, 23.
M. magnimamma. Black-tipped curved spines. Cream-white flowers. Widely available.
M. multiceps. Numerous soft white radial spines with reddish central spines. Widely available.
M. prolifera (little-candles, silver cluster cactus). Small globe-shaped with bristly white spines. Yellowish flowers. Available: 13, 16, 20, 22, 24, 31.
M. schiedeana. Cylindrical with many bristly yellow-tipped white spines. Widely available.
M. zeilmanniana (rose-pincushion). Solitary stems. Purple flowers. Widely available.

Mamillopsis
(mah-mill-*op*-sis)

FAMILY: Cactaceae
GROUP: Coryphantha
ORIGIN: Mexico

GENERAL DESCRIPTION:
The clustering light green stems of mamillopsis are barely visible through the numerous white spines, arranged in clusters at the tip of each tubercle. Thick mats of clumping stems can cover areas up to six feet around, each head measuring only 2" to 3" diameter.

FLOWER DESCRIPTION:
Red to orange funnelform flowers are borne near the tips of the stems in the spring. The blooms generally measure approximately 2" long and 2" wide.

PROPAGATION: Seed, cuttings.
CULTURE: General cactus culture. Avoid overpotting.

RECOMMENDED SPECIES:
M. senilis. Bristlelike white spines. Orange-yellow flowers. Available: 5, 13, 16, 22, 29, 31.

Myrtillocactus geometrizans

Melocactus
bahiensis

Neobesseya
missouriensis

Melocactus
(*mell*-oh-*kak*-tus)

FAMILY: Cactaceae
GROUP: Cactus
ORIGIN: Caribbean Islands, Mexico, Central and South America

GENERAL DESCRIPTION:
The prominently ribbed medium to dark green, oblong stems reach a maximum 18" diameter, 36" height, depending upon species. Clusters of yellow, reddish-brown or nearly black spines are located along the ribs. The melocactus is best noted for its cephalium, a densely woolly growth produced at the top of the plant after the stem has reached its mature size.

FLOWER DESCRIPTION:
Tiny pink, red or purplish flowers are borne on the cephalium during spring and summer. It takes a plant from 5 to 20 years to reach maturity and develop a cephalium, after which time it blooms.

PROPAGATION: Seed.
CULTURE: This shallow-rooted plant requires a shallow container and a loose, very well-drained soil. Feed frequently but very sparingly in summer. Cut down on water in winter. Specimens grown from seed are generally less temperamental and sensitive to cold.

RECOMMENDED SPECIES:
M. bahiensis. Straight brown spines. Low cephalium. Pinkish flowers. Available: 13, 15, 16, 21. 31.
M. intortus (turk's-cap cactus). Large-growing to 3' high. Long cephalium. Pinkish flowers. 13, 15, 20, 31.
M. matanzanus. Miniature variety, maximum 4" high. Matures in 4 to 5 years. Easiest to grow of genus. Available: 2, 5, 13, 15, 16.

Myrtillocactus
(murr-*till*-oh-kak-tus)

FAMILY: Cactaceae
GROUP: Cereus
ORIGIN: Mexico

GENERAL DESCRIPTION:
Tall, stout, branching stems often grow to a maximum height of 20' in habitat. Its blue-green stems are ribbed and have black spines.

FLOWER DESCRIPTION:
Clusters of small white flowers are borne on the areoles spring and summer.

PROPAGATION: Seed, cuttings.
CULTURE: General cactus culture. Young plants can be kept in containers. Mature specimens make dramatic landscape accents.

RECOMMENDED SPECIES:
M. geometrizans (blue-candle, blue-flame). The only species currently listed. Available: 9, 13, 15, 16.

Neobesseya
(nee-oh-*bess*-yuh)

FAMILY: Cactaceae
GROUP: Coryphantha
ORIGIN: Missouri River basin, Texas

GENERAL DESCRIPTION:
Generally considered a subgenus of coryphantha, the neobesseya is characterized by dull green clumping globular stems divided into irregular tubercles. While the clumps of stems can grow to be very large, individual heads seldom exceed 2" diameter. Neobesseya has semistiff 1"-long, brownish spines.

FLOWER DESCRIPTION:
The 2"-long funnelform blooms have pale yellow inner petals, a beautiful fringe of brownish-green petals on the outside. They appear at the apex of the plant in spring.

PROPAGATION: Seed.
CULTURE: General cactus culture. Recommended for more experienced growers as neobesseya is frequently difficult to re-establish.

RECOMMENDED SPECIES:
N. missouriensis (*Coryphantha missouriensis*). The only species still referred to as neobesseya. Available: 13, 20, 22, 31.

Neochilenia napina

Neoporteria subgibbosa

Notocactus
haselbergii

Neochilenia
(*nee*-oh-chil-*een*-eeah)

FAMILY: Cactaceae
GROUP: Echinocactus
ORIGIN: Chile

GENERAL DESCRIPTION:
Like the closely related neoporteria, members of this genus are globular to cylindrical plants reaching a maximum height of 10". The stems are often a dark purple-brown, tubercled, armed with many short horn-brown to brown spines.

FLOWER DESCRIPTION:
The bell-shaped purple-red and green flowers measure 1¼" to 2" long, appear near the top of the stems in the spring and summer.

PROPAGATION: Seed, occasionally by offsets.
CULTURE: General cactus culture. Moderately easy to grow.

RECOMMENDED SPECIES:
N. fulva 'aerocarpa'. Available: 5, 8, 13, 29.
N. napina. Spiraling tubercles. Black spines. Yellow flowers. Available: 5, 8, 13, 23, 26, 29, 31.
N. wagenknechtii 'multi flora'. Available: 5, 8, 20, 29.

Neoporteria
(nee-oh-pohr-*tair*-yuh)

FAMILY: Cactaceae
GROUP: Echinocactus
ORIGIN: Chile

GENERAL DESCRIPTION:
The green short-cylindrical stems of neoporteria are covered with many spines. The ribs have separate tubercles. The entire plant grows to a maximum height of 10 inches.

FLOWER DESCRIPTION:
Pinkish bell-shaped flowers measure 1½" long, are borne several at a time from one aerole in December, January and February.

PROPAGATION: Seed.
CULTURE: General cactus culture. These winter bloomers need generous culture from November to March, a rest period during our spring and summer.

RECOMMENDED SPECIES:
N. gerocephala (*N. nidus, N. senilis*). Densely covered with curved, white, needle-shaped spines. Pink flowers. Widely available.
N. nidus. See: *N. gerocephala.*
N. senilis. See: *N. gerocephala.*
N. subgibbosa. Many needle-shaped brownish spines. Pink or red flowers. Available: 15, 16, 20, 23, 29, 31.

Notocactus
(*no*-toh-*kak*-tus)

FAMILY: Cactaceae
GROUP: Echinocactus
ORIGIN: Brazil, Argentina, Paraguay

GENERAL DESCRIPTION:
The dark green globe-shaped to cylindrical stems of notocactus have rounded ribs, grow to a maximum height of 10 inches. Some species are covered with fine white spines, others have sharp, stiff yellowish to brown spines.

FLOWER DESCRIPTION:
Most plants have yellow flowers, a few red-purple. Generally speaking, they are bell-shaped, measuring from 1" to 3", appearing at the apex of the cactus in the summer.

PROPAGATION: Seed.
CULTURE: General cactus culture. An easy-to-grow cactus, good for beginners.

RECOMMENDED SPECIES:
N. apricus. Short globe-shaped with 3" long yellow flowers. Available: 5, 13, 15, 16, 22.
N. graessneri. Solitary thick stems with needle-shaped, glassy-yellow spines. Yellowish-green flowers. Available: 5, 8, 20, 23, 24, 28.
N. haselbergii (scarlet barrel cactus). Orange to red flowers bloom in January to February. Widely available.
N. ottonis. Needle-shaped yellow or brown spines. Yellow flowers. Widely available.

Opuntia microdasys
'Albispina'

Pachypodium species

Pachyphytum hybrid

Opuntia
(oh-*poon*-tee-uh)

FAMILY: Cactaceae
GROUP: Opuntia
ORIGIN: North, Central and
South America.

GENERAL DESCRIPTION:
This large and varied genus is characterized by three different sizes
and shapes of stems; flat oval pads to
12" across long; thin stems to 4' or
5' in length; or small, globular stems
to 3" diameter. The skin is generally
green, though a few species' are
purple. Spination on pad-shaped
leaves is usually a cluster of straight
spines, bristly to stout, dotted across
the surface. Tubular and globular
plants have varied spine sizes
and arrangements.

FLOWER DESCRIPTION:
Large bell-shaped flowers range
in color from mostly yellow to orange
or purple or white. On pad-shaped
species, they are on the circum-
ference of the stems. Tubular and
globular species bear their flowers
from areoles.

PROPAGATION: Seed, cuttings.
CULTURE: Many opuntia are cold-
hardy, and can be used in the
landscape in most parts of the U.S.

RECOMMENDED SPECIES:
O. basilaris (beaver-tail). Gray-green
to purplish pads. Reddish flowers.
Available: 4, 13, 17, 16.
O. microdasys (rabbit-ears, bunny-
ears). Yellowish-green pads with tufts
of yellow spines. Yellow flowers.
'Albispina' (polka-dot cactus). Tufts of
white spines. 'Rufida' (cinnamon
cactus, red bunny-ears). Tufts of red
spines. All widely available.

Oreocereus
see: Borzicactus

Pachyphytum
(pah-kee-*fie*-tum)

FAMILY: Crassulaceae
ORIGIN: Mexico

GENERAL DESCRIPTION:
The fat, rounded leaves of pachyphytum form attractive rosettes on
long, succulent stems. Leaf color can
range from a dusty gray-pink to
glaucous blue. The diameter of each
rosette can be up to 8" across,
depending on species.

FLOWER DESCRIPTION:
Small, bell-shaped flowers are borne
on a pendant stalk in spring and
summer. Color ranges from white to
orange to red or pink.

PROPAGATION: Cuttings, seed.
CULTURE: General succulent culture.
Pachyphytums need plenty of bright,
but not burning, sun to bring out
maximum foliar color. Their long
stems make them good hanging
basket subjects.

RECOMMENDED SPECIES:
P. 'Blue Haze.' Thickly succulent
bluish leaves. Available: 18, 20, 21,
24, 35, 36.
P. compactum (thick plant). Rounded,
very succulent leaves, whitish with
a nearly lavender hue. Available: 18,
20, 21, 22, 24, 31.

Pachypodium
(pah-kee-*poh*-dee-uhm)

FAMILY: Apocynaceae
ORIGIN: South Africa, Angola,
Madagascar

GENERAL DESCRIPTION:
This widely varied genus includes
plants that are shrubby, have tuberous
root systems, or are columnar and
covered with thorns, not unlike cacti.
The species with tuberous root
systems are generally those most
sought after by succulent collectors.
Most species have long, thin, leathery,
dark green, deciduous foliage.

FLOWER DESCRIPTION:
Flowers of pachypodium range from
white to yellow to red. The star-shaped
blooms, borne at the tips of the
branches, measure up to 2" across,
appearing in the spring.

PROPAGATION: Seed.
CULTURE: General succulent culture.
Pachypodiums go through a leafless
winter dormancy, when water should
be withheld. The tuberous root-stocks
of certain species make them
excellent bonsai subjects.

RECOMMENDED SPECIES:
P. lealii. Tuberous club-shaped trunk
with treelike branches that carry small
leaves, stout spines. White flowers.
Available: 7, 9, 15, 25, 31, 33.

P. rosulatum. Short, thick caudex
branching into spiny arms, topped by
foliage rosette. Bright yellow flowers
on long stalk. Available: 7, 9, 15, 33.
P. windsorii. (P. baronii: var, windsorii).
Dwarf caudex covered with rough
skin and tiny spines. Red flowers.
Available: 7, 9, 15, 33.

Parodia maassii

Pachyveria hybrid

Pelargonium species

X Pachyveria
(pah-kee-*vair*-yuh)

FAMILY: Crassulaceae
PARENTS: Echeveria x Pachyphytum

GENERAL DESCRIPTION:
This product of a bigeneric cross between echeveria and pachyphytum has produced a plant with the best characteristics of each parent.
X Pachyverias have the perfect rosette form of echeveria and stunning color range of pachyphytum.. The rosettes of succulent, glaucous leaves grow on rather long, succulent stems. Colors vary widely, including many shades of pink and luminous blues, grays, lavenders, and greens.

FLOWER DESCRIPTION:
Like its parents, X Pachyveria bears its bell-shaped flowers on a pendant stalk, mainly in spring and summer. Colors include yellow, orange, pink and red.

PROPAGATION: Cuttings.
CULTURE: General succulent culture.

RECOMMENDED SPECIES:
X *P. glauca.* Rosettes of glaucous leaves measuring to 4" across. Available: 20, 24.

X *P. haagei (jewel plant). Rosettes of bluish-green leaves with purplish-red at pointed tips. Available: 21, 22.*

Parodia
(pah-*roh*-dyuh)

FAMILY: Cactaceae
GROUP: Echinocactus
ORIGIN: Argentina, Bolivia, Paraguay, Brazil

GENERAL DESCRIPTION:
Small globular to cylindrical, light green stems are usually solitary, occasionally clustering. They grow to a maximum 3" diameter, 10" height, with ribs that are divided into spiralling tubercles. Parodia has many yellowish to red-brown spines.

FLOWER DESCRIPTION:
Brightly colored yellow to red flowers are borne in the yellowish wool at the plant's apex during the summer. Blooms are generally wide funnelform shape, measuring 1" to 2" long.

PROPAGATION: Seed.
CULTURE: General cactus culture. Prevent accumulation of water at collar of plant. Parodia's roots need an open, nourishing soil and even moisture during the growing season.

RECOMMENDED SPECIES:

P. aureispina (tom-thumb). Globe-shaped stems with bristly white spines. Yellow flowers.
Available: 2, 13, 15, 16, 22.

P. maassii. Solitary oval stems. Yellowish spines. Red flowers. Available: 16, 20, 28, 29, 31.

P. mutabilis. Many bristly white spines with stouter red to orange spines. Yellow flowers. Available: 16, 20, 22, 28, 31.

Pelargonium
(pell-ahr-*go*-nyum)

FAMILY: Geraniaceae
ORIGIN: South Africa, Madagascar

GENERAL DESCRIPTION:
The species most interesting to collectors have succulent, dark green stems sometimes armed with spines. Foliage is relatively sparse, green with lacy edges.

FLOWER DESCRIPTION:
Clusters of blooms resembling the genus' most popular member, common geraniums, appear on thin stems at the plant's tips. Colors range from white through pink, red, and purple; petals usually have darker markings. Bloom time is in spring and summer.

PROPAGATION: Cuttings.
CULTURE: General succulent culture. Species with thinner stems are generally easier to grow.

RECOMMENDED SPECIES:
P. echinatum (cactus geranium, sweethcart geranium) The easiest-to-grow succulent pelargonium. Available: 13, 16, 35, 36.

Pleiospilos species

Portulacaria afra 'Variegata'

Pelecyphora
aselliformis

Pelecyphora
(*pell*-eh-*siff*-ohr-uh)

FAMILY: Cactaceae
GROUP: Echinocactus
ORIGIN: Mexico

GENERAL DESCRIPTION:
The green, tubercled stems of pelecyphora grow either singly or in mat-forming clumps. They are globular to club-shaped (wider at the top than bottom). A distinctive feature of these cacti is their spinal arrangement. Elongated areoles are surrounded by short, white spines that are parallel with the plant's surface.

FLOWER DESCRIPTION:
Short tubular flowers are borne on the spine clusters below the top of the plant. The rose- to violet-colored flowers open during the day, close at night in the spring and summer. They measure up to 1¼" across.

PROPAGATION: Cuttings, seed.
CULTURE: General cactus culture.

RECOMMENDED SPECIES:
P. aselliformis (hatchet cactus). Columnar club-shaped stems to 4" high. Rose-colored flowers.
Available: 2, 13, 16, 22, 28, 29, 31.
P. strobiliformis. Depressed globular stems to 1½" high. Light to dark magenta flowers. Available: 13, 22, 31.

Pleiospilos
(plee-os-*py*-los)

FAMILY: Aizoaceae
ORIGIN: South Africa

GENERAL DESCRIPTION:
Thickly succulent, low-growing leaf pairs resemble small rocks. These membryanthemum mimicry plants are brown-gray with darker colored dots over the skin. They grow in stemless clumps that range in size from 1" to 5" in diameter.

FLOWER DESCRIPTION:
Yellow-orange dandelionlike flowers emerge from between the leaves in the summer. Blossoms are usually 2" to 3" across.

PROPAGATION: Seed.
CULTURE: General mesembryanthemum culture. Though more challenging than many succulents, pleiospilos is generally easier to grow than most mesembryanthemums.

RECOMMENDED SPECIES:
P. bolusii (mimicry plant, living-rock cactus). Gray-green or brownish skin with many dark green dots. Bright yellow flowers. Available: 5, 7, 13, 16, 18, 36:
P. nelii (splitrock, cleftstone). Dark gray-green or reddish leaves. Salmon-pink-yellow flowers. Available: 5, 7, 13, 16, 18.

Portulacaria
(pohr-too-lah-*kahr*-yuh)

FAMILY: Portulaceae
ORIGIN: South Africa

GENERAL DESCRIPTION:
A monotypic shrub, with reddish-brown trunk and stems and small, succulent green leaves.

FLOWER DESCRIPTION:
Clusters of small, pale pink flowers are produced by very old specimens. Younger plants do not flower.

PROPAGATION: Cuttings.
CULTURE: General succulent culture. A very easy-to-grow plant. The attractive reddish-brown stems and shrubby habit make protulacaria an ideal bonsai specimen.

RECOMMENDED SPECIES:
P. afra (elephant bush). Green leaves. 'Variegata'. Light green and creamy white variegated foliage. Both widely available in catalogs and retail nurseries.

Rebutia hybrid

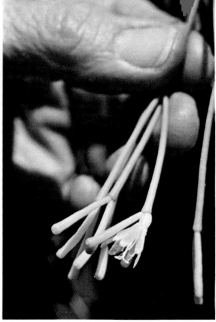

Schlumbergera hybrid

Rhipsallis
capilliformis

Rebutia
(reh-*boot*-yuh)

FAMILY: Cactaceae
GROUP: Lobivia
ORIGIN: Argentina, Bolivia, Paraguay

GENERAL DESCRIPTION:
Rebutias are small globe-shaped light green to dark shiny green cacti covered with many small, wartlike tubercles. The short spines range from white to dark brown.

FLOWER DESCRIPTION:
Large yellow, red or purple flowers make this genus a popular collector's item. From 5 to 20 very long, thin, funnelform flowers open from the base of the plant during the summer, often obscuring the cactus itself.

PROPAGATION: Seed and offsets.
CULTURE: General cactus culture. These free-blooming cacti are good for beginners. They remain small enough to suit the narrowest window-sill. Rebutias prefer filtered sun.

RECOMMENDED SPECIES:
R. deminuta. Brown-tipped or brown spines. Large dark orange-red flowers. Available: 13, 16, 18, 28.
R. grandiflora (scarlet crown cactus). Crimson flowers to 2½" long. Available: 13, 16, 21, 24, 28.
R. krainziana. Woolly areoles, white spines. Red to crimson flowers. Available: 5, 8, 15, 16, 22.
R. kupperana. Radial brown spines. Orange-red flowers. Available: 13, 15, 16, 18, 28.
R. minuscula (red-crown). Bristly white spines. Crimson flowers. Widely available.
R.senilis (fire-crown cactus). Carmine-red flowers. Widely available.

Rhipsalis
(*ripp*-sahl-u hs)

FAMILY: Cactaceae
GROUP: Cereus
ORIGIN: Central and South America

GENERAL DESCRIPTION:
The jointed, branching, leafless stems of rhipsalis cascade or climb in their native habitat. These epiphytes have aerial roots on their flattened or cylindrical green stems. They are generally spineless; a few species having insignificant bristles at eh aeroles.

FLOWER DESCRIPTION:
Flower shape, color, and size vary greatly within the genus. Some species have lovely small bell-shaped blossoms ranging from white to red; many have tiny, nondescript flowers, their yellowish-greens blending in with the stems. The fruits are small, nearly transparent berries, appearing almost like milk glass beads.

PROPAGATION: Cuttings, seed.
CULTURE: General tropical cactus culture. Rhipsalis is particularly well-suited to hanging basket culture.

RECOMMENDED SPECIES:
R. capilliformis. Thin, jointed, branching green stems. Small cream-colored flowers. Available: 11, 22, 30, 35.

Schlumbergera
(schlum-*bur*-gur-ah)

FAMILY: Cactaceae
GROUP: Hylocereus
ORIGIN: Brazil

GENERAL DESCRIPTION:
The flat, jointed stems of this genus have scalloped edges and short, inconspicuous bristles. The stems grow in segments, forming a sort of chain from the plant's trunk.

FLOWER DESCRIPTION:
Schlumbergeras are cultivated for their numerous winter flowers. The blossoms are hooded; bright shades of red. They are borne on the ends of the jointed stems.

PROPAGATION: Cuttings, seed.
CULTURE: General tropical cactus culture. The schlumbergera's winter bloom cycle requires more water during November to March, tapering off April through September. They make ideal hanging basket specimens and do well as houseplants.

RECOMMENDED SPECIES:
S. bridgesii (Christmas cactus). Cerise flowers on stems to 1" long. Widely available in retail nurseries and through catalogs.
S. truncata (Thanksgiving cactus, crab cactus). Similar to *S. bridgesii*, but with scallop-edged stems, irregular flowers. Widely available in retail nurseries and through catalogs.

Far left:
Sedum x rubrotinctum
Left:
Sedum morganianum

Below:
Selenicereus
hybrid

Sempervivum tectorum

Sedum
(*see*-duhm)

FAMILY: Crassulaceae
ORIGIN: Northern temperate regions, parts of Africa and South America.

GENERAL DESCRIPTION:
Very few generalizations can be made about this large, varied genus. The succulent foliage comes in many colors and forms, including vining, creeping, and upright shrubby growth.

FLOWER DESCRIPTION:
Sedums produce small flowers in colors ranging from white and yellow to dusty pink or deep rose. The small blossoms generally cluster on a short stem above the foliage.

PROPAGATION: Cuttings, seed.
CULTURE: General succulent culture. Sedums are among the easiest to grow of the succulent genera. Many species and varieties are cold-hardy, making them excellent outdoor plants in cold-winter regions.

RECOMMENDED SPECIES:
S. morganianum (burro's-tail). Succulent light green leaves cluster on hanging stems. Frost-tender. Widely available.
S. oxypetalum. Shrubby plant, to 5' tall. The bark on its trunk peels. Reddish flowers appear after leaves drop. Widely available.
S. x rubrotinctum (Christmas-cheer). Small, very succulent leaves on short stems. Light green foliage becomes red when grown in full sun. A good ground cover in frost-free areas. Widely available.
S. spathulifolium. Rosettes of tiny dark green outer leaves with grayish inner leaves on short, draping stems. An attractive container plant or ground cover. Widely available.

Selenicereus
(sell-en-ee-*seer*-yus)

FAMILY: Cactaceae
GROUP: Hylocereus
ORIGIN: Caribbean islands, tropical Mexico and Central America

GENERAL DESCRIPTION:
Climbing or hanging stems can measure up to 15' long. They are slender (½" to 1½" thick), cylindrical, green when young, turning purple as they age. Depending upon the species, some stems are tubular, others ribbed or angular. Short, bristly spines are borne in clusters on the areoles of most species. The stems produce air roots, intended for grasping the trees that selenicereus climbs in its native habitat.

FLOWER DESCRIPTION:
Large funnelform flowers are borne along the stems. The white blossoms measure up to 8" long, to 10" across. The blooms open evenings in summer.

PROPAGATION: Seed, Cuttings.
CULTURE: General tropical cactus culture. Due to its climbing growth habit, selenicereus must be given adequate room. Well suited to hanging basket culture.

RECOMMENDED SPECIES:
S. grandiflorus (queen-of-the-night). Ribbed stems. White flowers 7" to 10" long. Widely available.
S. pteranthus (princess-of-the-night). Prominently ribbed stems. Fragrant flowers. Available: 9, 18, 21, 22.

Sempervivum
(semm-pur-*vee*-vuhm)

FAMILY: Crassulaceae
ORIGIN: Mountains of Europe, Asia and Africa.

GENERAL DESCRIPTION:
This large genus is characterized by small rosette-shaped plants that grow in mat-forming clumps. The nearly stemless leaves have pointed ends and come in a vast array of colors, including every shade of green and some very dramatic reds and purples. The succulent rosettes seldom exceed 3" across and are often covered with small hairs, sometimes numerous enough to give the appearance of spider webs.

FLOWER DESCRIPTION:
The flower color of sempervivum varies widely. The small blossoms are borne on a stalk that pushes out of the rosette's center in spring or summer.

PROPAGATION: Cuttings, division, seed.
CULTURE: General succulent culture. Sempervivums are easy to grow and have an extra advantage — many species and varieties are winter-hardy. They can be planted outdoors in cold-winter areas with minimal protection.

RECOMMENDED SPECIES:
S. arachnoideum (cobweb houseleek). Tiny, dense rosettes of green leaves with many fine hairs. Bright red flowers. Widely available.
S. 'Clara Noyes'. Lovely rosettes of deep red, succulent leaves. Available: 15, 19, 29.
S. tectorum (common houseleek). Widely opened, green rosette, often tipped with purple. Widely available.

Senecio
rowleyanus

Senecio
haworthii

Stapelia x pasadenensis

Setiechinopsis
mirabilis

Senecio
(sen-*ess*-yoh)

FAMILY: Compositae
ORIGIN: Worldwide

GENERAL DESCRIPTION:
This large and widely varied genus includes species whose growth habits range from small succulents, to hanging or climbing vines, to large shrubs. The white-felted to green to bluish-green stems are spineless, supporting leaves that are spherical, thickly succulent or flat and elongated.

FLOWER DESCRIPTION:
Small daisylike flowers come in yellows, whites, and reds, depending upon species. Some are petalless; all are small, seldom exceeding 1" across. They are borne at the ends of the stems in summer.

PROPAGATION: Cuttings, seed.
CULTURE: General succulent culture. Very easy to grow.

RECOMMENDED SPECIES:
S. haworthii (cocoon plant). Small succulent shrub with soft, feltlike hairs on leaves. Yellow-orange flowers. Available: 7, 15, 22, 31, 36.
S. herreianus (gooseberry kleinia). Hanging or climbing vine with thickly succulent eliptical green leaves. Excellent hanging basket specimen. Available: 13, 15, 16, 22, 29, 31, 35, 36.
S. rowleyanus (string-of-beads). Spherical green leaves on hanging or climbing vine. A beautiful hanging basket subject. Widely available.

Setiechinopsis
(sett-ee-*eck*-in-*opp*-sis)

FAMILY: Cactaceae
GROUP: Cereus
ORIGIN: Argentina

GENERAL DESCRIPTION:
A monotypic, small, ribbed cactus characterized by solitary, slender stems to 1" diameter, 6" long. Each stem has 11 ribs and short, bristly brown spines.

FLOWER DESCRIPTION:
White flowers, measuring 2" across, are borne on a very long, thin tube from the top of the plant. Blooming occurs in late spring and summer.

PROPAGATION: Seed.
CULTURE: General cactus culture. A good container plant.

RECOMMENDED SPECIES:
S. mirabilis. Available: 15, 16, 23, 29, 31.

Stapelia
(stah-*peel*-ya)

FAMILY: Asclepiadaceae
ORIGIN: Africa, Asia

GENERAL DESCRIPTION:
Stapelia stems are from ½" to 1" diameter and grow in clusters to 2' long. The gray-green to dark, brownish-green stems are leafless, but have soft teeth on their margins.

FLOWER DESCRIPTION:
Stapelias are grown for their large (1" to 5" across) 5-lobed starfish-shaped flowers. The showy blossoms, generally yellowish, splotched with maroon or brown, are borne along the stems. Blooming occurs from summer to autumn, each flower lasting approximately 2 days. The flowers are carion-scented as a means of attracting the flies that pollinate the plant. As such, it is best grown in a place where the beautiful blooms can be seen but not smelled.

PROPAGATION: Seed, offsets, cuttings.
CULTURE: General stapeliad culture. Stapelias need very loose, porous soil. They will rot if kept too wet, be attacked by mealybugs if too dry and they benefit from frequent re-potting. Water very sparingly in cold weather. Not recommended for beginners.

RECOMMENDED SPECIES:
S. hirsuta (hairy toad plant). Cream or yellowish and dark purple-brown flowers. Available: 9, 13, 16, 18, 20, 22, 24, 33.
S. x pasadenensis. Wine-red flowers. Available: 7, 16, 18, 22.
S. verrucosa. Flowers are pale yellow spotted with blood-red. Available: 7, 13, 16, 20, 22.

Strombocactus
see: Turbinicarpus

Thelocactus nidulans

Tillandsia xerographica

Sulcorebutia species

Sulcorebutia
(sull-co-reh-*bue*-tyah)

FAMILY: Cactaceae
GROUP: Lobivia
ORIGIN: South America

GENERAL DESCRIPTION:
The globular tubercled stems of sulcorebutia are generally small growers, seldom exceeding 2" to 3" diameter. They cluster as the plants mature. Sulcorebutias are most easily distinguished from rebutias by their elongated areoles and short, recurved spines.

FLOWER DESCRIPTION:
Sulcorebutias bear large funnelform flowers in spring and early summer. Their colors range from bright yellows and deep gold to red and orange. While rebutias produce flowers only from the base of the stems, sulcorebutias carry blossoms on any of the lower areoles.

PROPAGATION: Seed, cuttings.
CULTURE: General cactus culture. These petite, colorful bloomers make ideal windowsill specimens.

RECOMMENDED SPECIES:
S. caniguerallii. Approximately 1" diameter heads with very dark brownish green stems and very short pectinate spines. Reddish flowers with yellow throat. Available: 31, 36.
S. crispata. Globose heads to 2" diameter. Light green body, tenuous honey colored spines to ¼" long. Bright pink flowers. Available: 31, 36.
S. glomeriseta. Deep green body to 2" diameter with black spines. Flowers of brilliant cerise. Available: 31, 36.

Thelocactus
(*thell*-oh-kak-tus)

FAMILY: Cactaceae
GROUP: Coryphantha
ORIGIN: Mexico

GENERAL DESCRIPTION:
Thelocactus is characterized by small-growing, depressed, globular, or occasionally cylindrical stems, most measuring under 7" high. The bright green to gray-green stems are divided into tubercles which are, in some species, united to form ribs. Spines ranging in color from brown and gray to white, yellow, and red, are clustered at the tubercle tips.

FLOWER DESCRIPTION:
Widely opened bell-shaped flowers are borne on the top of the plant, in colors ranging from yellow to red-pink. Bloom occurs in spring.

PROPAGATION: Seed.
CULTURE: General cactus culture. These plants are most responsive to slightly drier than average culture, and to a soil mix that includes a little gypsum.

RECOMMENDED SPECIES:
T. bicolor (glory-of-Texas). Purple flowers on conical stems. Available: 2, 9, 13, 16.
T. leucanthus. Clustering stems with yellow to gray spines, yellow flowers. Available: 13, 16, 23, 28, 31.
T. nidulans. Solitary stems with brown spines, yellowish-white flowers. Available: 9, 16, 24, 28.

Tillandsia
(till-*ahnz*-yuh)

FAMILY: Bromeliaceae
ORIGIN: Tropical regions of the Americas

GENERAL DESCRIPTION:
The long, curving spindle- to triangular-shaped leaves of tillandsia form a rosette, occasionally on a stem. These epiphytes have aerial roots for gripping trees, rock cliffs, or similar support in their native habitat. Unlike succulents, they do not store water in their stems and leaves; they survive on what little moisture is borne through the air. The foliage is often an attractive silvery color, with highlights of pink to pale orange.

FLOWER DESCRIPTIONS:
Clusters of small blue, green, purple, red, orange, or white flowers are borne on a stalk.

PROPAGATION: Division.
CULTURE: Dry-growing tillandsias are best mounted on a piece of plain wood, cork bark, or Guatemalan tree fern bark (available from specialty nurseries). Plants should be misted in warm dry weather to ensure adequate moisture.

RECOMMENDED SPECIES:
T. ionantha. Dwarf rosette of green outer leaves, pink or red inner leaves. Violet flowers. Available: 1, 6, 12, 17, 32, 35.
T. usneoides (Spanish moss). Many-branched, leafy, hanging stems. Silvery-gray. Common in the southern United States. Available: 1, 32.

Trichocereus hybrid

Trichodiadema bulbosum

Turbinicarpus species

Trichocereus
(tree-ko-*seer*-yus)

FAMILY: Cactaceae
GROUP: Cereus
ORIGIN: Andes Mountains, from Chile and northwestern Argentina through Bolivia and Peru to Ecuador.

GENERAL DESCRIPTION:
Members of this genus range from plants with tall, branching, columnar stems to procumbent, creeping cacti that can stretch as far as 20 or 30 feet. The prominently ribbed green stems have clusters of stout yellow-brown or gray spines along their ribs.

FLOWER DESCRIPTION:
Most species have large, fragrant, white, funnelform flowers. Blooms measuring up to 8" across open from areoles all along the stems in summer.

PROPAGATION: Seed, cuttings.
CULTURE: General cactus culture. These cacti make good landscape specimens in frost-free areas, tolerating greater than average water and low-nitrogen fertilizers.

RECOMMENDED SPECIES:
T. pachanoi. Tall upright branching stems. Fragrant white flowers. Available: 13, 16, 20, 23, 25.
T. spachianus (torch cactus). Shorter upright branching stems. Fragrant white flowers. Widely available.

Trichodiadema
(*tree*-koh-*dee*-ah-*dee*-mah)

FAMILY: Aizoaceae
ORIGIN: South Africa, Ethiopa

GENERAL DESCRIPTION:
Members of this genus tend to grow as shrubby or short-stemmed succulents. The longer-stemmed plants are often used as ground covers in frost-free areas. The shorter-stemmed species have thick, tuberous roots. All species have small, spindle-shaped, green to gray-green leaves with small spinelike bristles at their tops.

FLOWER DESCRIPTION:
Small daisylike flowers appear in early summer near the end of the stems. Their colors include bright magenta, brilliant reddish-purple, white, and yellow.

PROPAGATION: Seed, cuttings.
CULTURE: General succulent culture. Most growth occurs in summer. Plants respond well to diluted applications of low-nitrogen fertilizer and frequent pruning. Tuberous-rooted plants make excellent bonsai subjects.

RECOMMENDED SPECIES:
T. bulbosum. Light tan, thick, tuberous roots. Magenta flowers. Available: 13, 16, 20, 22.
T. densum. Tuberous roots. Tiny, succulent, green stems. Carmine flowers. Widely available.

Turbinicarpus
(toor-bin-nih-*kahr*-pus)

FAMILY: Cactaceae
GROUP: Echinocactus
ORIGIN: Mexico

GENERAL DESCRIPTION:
The round, disclike stems of turbinicarpus are made up of irregularly shaped tubercles that range in color from blue-gray to blue-green to gray-green. Wider than it is high, slow growing and always solitary, the turbinicarpus seldom exceeds a 1" to 3" diameter or grows taller than 1." Most species have weak straight or curved spines in clusters on the areoles. A few develop hair or wool.

FLOWER DESCRIPTION:
Measuring ½" to 1½" across, the short-tubed wide-funnelform flowers are large in proportion to the plant. They are white with purple markings and appear at the center of the cactus in late summer.

PROPAGATION: Seed.
CULTURE: General cactus culture. Best if grown in a container, but avoid overpotting. Winter watering must be very light.

RECOMMENDED SPECIES:
T. psuedomacrochele (*Strombo-cactus psuedomacrochele*). Stiff, twisted gray spines. Available: 15, 16, 28, 31.
T. schmiedickeanus (*Strombocactus schmiedickeanus*). Curved brown spines. Rose-colored flowers. Available: 5, 8, 15, 16.

Culture and propagation

Succulents are remarkably easy to grow. By observing a few simple rules and procedures, it is possible to enjoy a healthy and attractive collection. This chapter gives you the information you'll need to start and maintain your succulent plants.

Good cultural practices start before you bring your succulents home to your collection. One of the best ways to be sure you have a happy, healthy collection is to buy healthy plants, either from a retail dealer or a reputable mail-order nursery.

When choosing a plant at the nursery or plant shop, take a good look at it; you want to bring home the healthiest specimens you can find. Look for the sturdiest plant, not the biggest. Give it a gentle tug to see if it's well rooted. Be sure it has no broken or scarred leaves. Check for insect pests such as mealy bug or scale. When you get your plant home, knock it out of the pot and take a look at the soil.

Succulents are often potted in lightweight soil mixes for shipping and handling. They are adequate to maintain the plant during the distribution process from grower to retailer to you but plants might need to be repotted with another rooting medium before they become a permanent part of your collection. Because succulents are frequently top-heavy, sometimes plaster of Paris has been used to stabilize the plant to prevent its being damaged if knocked over. If your plant is firmly embedded in a hard, white lump, that's plaster of Paris. It's water soluble, so just take the plant out of the pot and soak the root ball until the plaster of Paris comes apart. Once the root system can be worked free, repot the plant in the soil mix appropriate to the species. (See charts, pp. 94-95).

If you buy from specialty nurseries that stock *only* succulents, their plants will probably be properly potted in appropriate soil mix and pot. Mail-order specialty nurseries are a good source for hard-to-find varieties. Plants are often sent bareroot along with instructions for potting and maintenance. They must be potted up as soon as they are received. The best way to find a reliable mail-order source is to check with other collectors in your area for recommendations. If the source is unfamiliar, place only a small test order. If you find the plants and service satisfactory, it will probably be as good on a more extensive order. Shipped plants are usually small, and for good reason — younger plants are easier to re-establish in a new environment. They develop new roots sooner and grow faster than mature plants of the same species. A fully mature, ready-to-bloom plant takes much longer to readjust and, under less than expert care might not survive the transition.

Soil mixes

Most successful collectors keep two or three containers of prepared soil mixes, or the ingredients for soil mixes, readily available for short-notice potting jobs. Kept in covered containers, protected from soil pests and excess moisture, the prepared soils, or their ingredients, are ready and waiting when new arrivals turn up. A stock pile of clean, sterilized pots in a variety of sizes and a trowel complete the list of useful items to have on hand for potting.

To keep succulents healthy, a soil mix must comprise three essentials: moisture retention, drainage (aeration), and nourishment. The soil must retain sufficient moisture to dissolve nutrients so they can be absorbed by the roots.

Drainage is the soil's ability to drain off excess moisture immediately in order to provide for adequate aeration. Roots need a balance of both water and air in the soil to survive. With too much water the roots "drown" and rot, with too little, the roots starve and the plant dehydrates. Either extreme will kill the plant. If, however, you are inclined toward extremes, it is preferable with succulents to sin in the direction of too little water than too much. The formulas given for soil mixes in this chapter will assure you of a fast-draining, well-aerated soil.

The third element, nourishment, is the variable. Although all succulents must have adequate moisture and excellent aeration, they vary in the amount of nourishment they require. As a rule, the jungle species (tropical epiphytes such as *rhipsalis* or *epiphyllums*) require a richer soil than the desert, alpine, or shoreline species. A few — and these are a small minority of succulents — thrive best in a very lean or low-nutrient growing medium. The cultural charts on pages 94-95 indicate which soil mix is appropriate to each species.

You could talk to ten experienced growers and come up with ten different formulas for soil mixes for succulents. To forestall this we describe three basic ingredients and the purposes they serve. We'll suggest acceptable substitutes, some of which might be available in your area. You may never have heard of some of them before but all of them have their advocates, and you can take your choice in terms of cost and availability.

Potting soil as a basic

The base for almost any potting mix is soil. Use any packaged sterilized potting soil. There are several brands, all equally good. You can find them

Undaunted by the spines, a bee pollinates a mammillaria blossom: Nature's way of assuring the continuance of a species.

at garden centers and nurseries. They have the advantages of coming in convenient sizes and being disease-, pest-, and weed-free. Consider a packaged soil your basic ingredient, but not a complete soil. It retains too much moisture for succulents when used by itself. You can substitute good garden loam if you have it available, or your local nursery may offer its own sterilized garden soil, which will do as well.

Testing drainage

Coarse sand is an ingredient used to provide aeration and drainage. It is often available at builder's supply centers. Be sure to get a coarse grade; fine sand packs down hard, eliminating air spaces. It also crusts over on the surface, making it hard for water to penetrate. Don't use beach sand; it's much too fine and too salty.

Many growers use sponge rock to provide drainage and aeration because it is lightweight and does not compact. The soil remains porous and fast-draining. Succulents are, as a rule, slow growing plants and do not need to be repotted frequently unless the soil compacts and drainage becomes poor.

Sponge rock does have one inconvenient feature; it is so lightweight that it floats off the surface of the soil when you water. As a result, some growers prefer a fine-grade crushed volcanic rock which is slightly heavier. Like sponge rock, it does not break down in the soil and will provide fast drainage over a period of years. It is available at garden centers in either black or red and, except for the color, there is no difference between the two.

Other substitutes for coarse sand are perlite, silt-free decomposed granite, and coarsely crushed charcoal. Pet stores carry activated charcoal in small amounts, and farm supply stores stock poultry charcoal. Agricultural pumice (mined from an area in the California desert) is preferred by many commercial succulent growers instead of coarse sand or perlite. It does not break down, so permanently prohibits soil shrinkage or compacting. It is stable in the pot, not floating like perlite or washing down like sand.

The last essential ingredient is leaf mold (compost). This gives the potting mix bulk and texture and releases nutrients to the plant over a considerable period of time. If you have a yard, a compost heap will provide you with a free supply from your garden leftovers — leaves, grass clippings, any vegetable kitchen waste. If leaf mold isn't available, you can substitute sphagnum moss; you'll find it at nurseries and garden centers. Note: sphagnum moss and peat moss are not the same, and peat moss will not do. It's too acidic, it compacts, and it retains moisture too long.

Using these ingredients, you can make up a potting soil that will suit any succulent by varying the proportions of each ingredient. The three soil mixes recommended here will take care of the needs of a wide variety of species. Check the cultural charts on pages 94-95 for the mixture appropriate to the plant you're potting up.

Basic recipes

#1 Extra-lean
(A very low-nutrient formula)
2 parts coarse sand or
  Agricultural pumice
1 part potting soil

#2 Regular
(A general formula)
1 part coarse sand or
  Agricultural pumice
1 part potting soil
1 part leaf mold

#3 Extra-rich
(A high-nutrient formula)
1 part coarse sand or
  Agricultural pumice
1 part potting soil
2 parts leaf mold

Something to pot it in

New plastic or glazed pots can be used immediately but new clay pots should be soaked before using to keep the pot from absorbing water from the soil.

Used pots should be scrubbed and sterilized. Scrubbing is considerably easier if you soak the pot before you start to scrub and sterilizing can be done in a jiffy on the dry cycle in the dishwasher.

If you use bleach or some chemical to sterilize your pots, be sure to rinse them thoroughly before using them. One cactus expert who uses clay pots exclusively soaks them in rainwater for 24 hours after sterilizing them chemically. Nonporous pots, such as plastic or glazed containers, do not need soaking after sterilizing because they do not absorb the chemicals that can burn the roots.

The size of the pot is determined by the shape and size of the plant. Tall, shrubby, or cylindrical plants should have pots half as wide as the height of the plant. An 8″ plant should have a pot 4″ in diameter. Globular plants should have a pot one inch wider around than the plant. A golden barrel cactus twelve inches across needs a 13″ pot. (The size of a pot is determined by its diameter.)

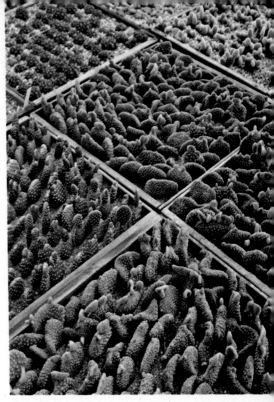

Like a complex mosaic, stem cuttings root in flats at a commercial nursery.

It's not always possible to find a pot precisely the right size, but come as close as possible. The plant needs room for root growth and space for watering at the top. You can compensate for an oversized pot by adding more drainage material in the soil mixture. This insures that the soil will not remain too wet too long.

To assure a long and healthy life for your plants, keep these factors in mind when choosing a container:

1. Size of the pot should be compatible with the size and shape of the plant.
2. Porous pots (clay) dry out more quickly that nonporous pots.
3. The drainage hole should be adequate to allow fast drainage.

The potting process

Potting is much easier when your materials are organized and you follow the routine outlined below.

✓ Check your new plant for pests to be sure it's clean and healthy before introducing it to the rest of your collection.

✓ Prepare your soil mixture before unpotting your new plant.

✓ Choose a scrubbed, sterilized container. Cut a piece of wire mesh — old window screening is perfect — large enough to cover the drainage hole with an overlap of ¼″ all around. The purpose of the mesh is to allow water to drain out without washing away the soil. To hold the wire in place, bend a piece of flexible wire into a wide U-shape. Thread the ends through the mesh and drainage hole, then bend them in opposite directions on the bottom outside of the pot. Place a curved piece of broken clay pot over the screened drainage hole as an added precaution against soil washing out or clogging the screen and slowing down drainage.

✔ Moisten some potting mix slightly and make a small pad or layer of soil in the bottom of the pot. The soil should be crumbly damp, not soaked. Wet soil is an open invitation to root rot.

✔ Knock the plant out of the pot. Check the root ball for pests or damaged roots. Cut away any broken, dead, or diseased roots with a pair of sterilized pruning scissors like the ones florists use for cutting stems. Rub the shoulders of the root ball gently to remove the hard crust at the base of the stem. Squeeze the root ball gently to crumble away any soil not adhering to the roots.

Pick up the plant, supporting the stem so it doesn't break under its own weight.

Center the plant in the pot, making sure the soil does not cover the stem or trunk. Always maintain the same soil level at which the plant was growing before. Plan to leave one full inch of space between the soil level and the top of the pot so that the soil won't wash over the edge of the pot when you water.

Hold the plant in place with one hand and pour the soil evenly around the roots. A sugar or flour scoop is handy for this part of the job. If the plant is an uncomfortably prickly sort, leather gloves will protect your hands. A rolled newspaper folded around the plant will also work well. The best way to handle the armed varieties is with caution.

When the pot is filled with soil, take the pot in both hands and tap it gently on the potting table to settle the soil. Chopsticks work nicely to tamp the soil in among the roots. Use your thumbs to firm the soil into place, or a blunt stick if the plant is spiny. Once the plant is firmly entrenched, the potting job is done. Do not water. Wait several days before watering.

Top dressing
Some experts use a top dressing of pebbles or crushed rock to give their plants a neat, finished appearance and to prevent the soil surface from crusting. It also reduces the rate of evaporation, which means the soil remains moister longer — and therein lies the rub. There are two schools of thought on the use of top dressings. Some experts claim that it can cover up a watering problem — either too wet or too dry — and the top dressing makes it harder to check on the state of soil. In cool, moist climates it may contribute to the soil remaining damp enough to encourage root rot.

The opposite point of view is that top dressing prevents the soil from being splashed on the plant, allows water to penetrate slowly and evenly, keeps the soil from crusting over, and looks attractive.

Like clay pots or plastic pots, there are advantages and disadvantages to both methods; the important point is to be aware of the way in which a top dressing influences the cultural techniques. Plants with top dressing will need watering less often and dry out more slowly than those without top dressing. Plants without top dressing will dry out faster and need watering more frequently. Whichever way you choose, modify your watering habits accordingly.

Now that the potting is done, find a shady, protected place to tuck your plant for a few days. It will need some time to adjust and you will need some time to observe how it took the transplanting. If the plant looks healthy and well adjusted at the end of a week, water it and introduce it to the rest of the family. If the plant is to go into full sun, make the transition slowly, over a period of several days, moving it into a brighter position every couple of days — even the toughest plant will sunscald if it goes from shade to sun too quickly. (This is a warm-weather caution; winter sun is rarely a problem.)

It probably took you longer to read the instructions than it will take you to pot up plants, and if you follow the steps, you'll have sturdy, attractive specimens to show for your time.

Watering
Now that your newly acquired plant is comfortably situated in a new pot and the proper soil, it's time to learn about watering.

The beginner always asks, "How often should I water?"

Any horticulturist worth his salt will give you the infuriating, frustrating and only accurate answer, "It depends on the growing conditions."

Quite simply, all plants require both water and air around their roots. Too much water and they drown; too much air and they starve (dehydrate). By reviewing the following seven categories, weather, light, leaves, stems, roots, containers, and top dressings, you should be able to determine your own growing conditions and what the water requirements are for your individual plants.

Weather. If the weather is cool, moist, foggy or overcast, don't water. It is essential to avoid the death-dealing combination of moisture and low temperatures. Succulents rot easily under cool, damp conditions.

Hot weather and wind cause the plant to use up water in transpiration and they also dry out the soil. Some succulents have developed their own defenses against heat and drying winds such as the coarse heavy hairs of *Cephalocereus senilis* or the abundant spines of *Cleistocactus strausii* or the ground hugging habit of adromischus. In general, if the plant is looking plump and juicy, don't water it. Succulents are one of the few things to which the phrase "fat and happy" applies — if they're fat, they're happy. When new growth is visible, a little more frequent watering encourages it.

Light. The higher the light intensity (and the accompanying heat), the more water the plant can use because there is a greater loss of water from both transpiration and evaporation.

Plants in full sun need more water than plants in light shade. It is important to note that not all succulents prefer full sun; many species will sunscald or dehydrate in direct sun.

Even those that do well in full sun need to make the transition slowly if they have previously been grown in some shade or indoors.

Safety first

Thorny cacti can be safely handled with a band of folded newspaper.

Some plants will develop a reddish coloration in full sun, rather like a human tan. If the plant looks shrivelled or limp in hot weather, water it.

Leaves. Thick leaves and stems serve to store water for rainless periods. A thick, leathery skin on the leaf surface helps limit the amount of water loss from transpiration. Spines and hairs also help reduce the amount of evaporation.

The more leaves or the larger the leaves the plant has, the greater the water loss in hot or windy weather. If your plant has many thin leaves it will require more frequent watering than a plant that has no leaves and is covered with long, coarse hairs.

While this does not tell you exactly when or precisely how much to water your plant, it will give you an idea of how to group plants with similar watering needs as your collection grows.

Stems. The size and texture of the stems indicate whether or not the stems are capable of storing moisture and how vulnerable they are to the desiccating effects of dryness, heat, and wind.

Some succulents are little more than stems, their leaves having become modified into hairs or spines (many cacti and euphorbias). Others have a thin, leathery covering (such as *Crassula arborescens)* which reduces moisture loss from the stem. In general, the thicker and juicier the stem, the greater its capacity for storing moisture.

Roots. Plants with bulbous, coarse roots like those of *Trichodiadema bulbosum* and *Jatropha cathartica,* have a large water-storing capacity. In addition to the efficiency of its bulbous roots for storing moisture, *T. bulbosum* also has a tough outer covering over its roots and stems which aids in water retention. Its small fat leaves, though numerous, are covered with tiny hairs that are an added protection against excessive evaporation from the leaf surface.

J. cathartica has a large, round root above the soil surface that acts as a water tank, and feeder roots below the soil. Its precaution against water loss from its thin leaves is to drop both leaves and stems very soon after flowering and fruiting in summer, remaining entirely dormant until the following spring. The swollen, bulbous portion of the root that remains exposed to wind and weather has a hard, barklike surface that allows little moisture to escape.

Containers. The amount of moisture lost from the soil due to evaporation is determined to a large extent by the kind of container used.

Porous containers, such as common terra-cotta or red clay pots, allow water to evaporate through their sides, causing the soil in them to dry out faster than the soil in non-porous containers.

Nonporous containers, such as plastic, ceramic, or glazed pots, do not allow the evaporation of water through their sides, so the soil in them remains moist considerably longer.

Clay pots allow for better aeration of the soil but need more frequent watering. Nonporous pots require watering less often but require careful attention to prevent the combination of wet soil and low temperatures which permits the growth of fungi that cause succulents to rot. Both have their advantages and disadvantages; the important point is that each requires a different approach to growing succulents.

Top dressing. Both in the ground and in containers, soil surface evaporation can be reduced considerably by the use of a top dressing of pebbles, coarse gravel, or crushed rock.

A rule of thumb

By considering these seven factors you can determine reasonably well how often and how much to water your plants. If you are still not sure, insert your finger into the soil up to the first joint ,or use a slim stick such as a toothpick or the thin end of a chopstick to a depth of 1 inch. If the soil is dry one inch below the surface, water it. Watering should be done, generally speaking, after the soil has been allowed to dry out. As always, there are exceptions to every rule. Consult the charts on pages 94-95 for each species' requirements, keeping in mind that plants need more water during their active growing seasons.

How to water

How the water is applied is also important. The best way to water landscape plantings is by slow irrigation. The best way to water succulents in pots is to plunge them to the rim in a bucket of water and immerse them until they stop bubbling. The bubbles are from the air that is pushed to the surface of the soil as the water fills the air pockets in the soil. When the soil is saturated, set the pot on a wire rack or a bed of crushed rock or gravel to drain thoroughly. Don't set the pot in a saucer — the water may collect. Succulents don't like to sit in puddles — put them somewhere where the water can drain off freely.

As a general rule, overhead sprinkling is not a good way to water succulents. Excess moisture might remain on the plant, exposing it to rot and other forms of fungus. Regular overhead watering can remove the bloom (powder) that is an attractive feature of many succulents as well as a natural protection against excessive light absorption. The chemical salts present in many water sources can also cause spotting on foliage. Unfortunately, the damage is permanent. So be careful!

There are occasions when overhead sprinkling is beneficial. Done on warm summer mornings, it's a good way to rinse off dust and dirt and discourage summer pests. But be careful when spraying those plants that have a powdery coating that you don't spray too hard; the powder is not replaced if it is disturbed. Watering on warm mornings will permit the soil to dry out a little before temperatures drop in the evening.

Most tap water in this country is treated with chemicals to purify it. These chemicals can concentrate in the soil, especially in potted plants, and sometimes appear on the sides and rims of clay pots as crusty, white deposits. These salts can burn plant tissues, especially the delicate feeder roots, if they concentrate in the soil.

There are several ways to prevent this. You can allow tap water to stand overnight; the chemicals will evaporate out of the water. You can use rainwater, well water, or spring water, if one is available. Or, you can make a practice of leaching out your pots every third time you water. Leaching consists simply of pouring water through the soil from top to bottom and allowing it to drain at least three times. This rinses the salts out of the soil and out of the pores of porous pots.

The visible effects of salt burn on your plants are brown tips on the leaves. Salt burns can also damage roots and can weaken the whole plant. One important warning is in order: don't use chemically softened water on any plant. Softened water has an extremely high salt content and will damage your plants severely.

In general, water your plants thoroughly, and then let them dry out. Water early in the day so that most of the surface water will have evaporated by the time evening temperatures begin to drop. If you overhead-sprinkle, keep plants out of direct sun until the surface droplets evaporate. Remember that moisture and cool temperatures are an open invitation to various forms of rot.

Seedlings require a different watering program until they are well established. The care of young plants grown from seed is covered in the section on propagation (page 91).

As you become familiar with your plants, you will begin to recognize their needs simply by observing their general physical appearance. Succulents are wonderfully tolerant, even of novice gardeners.

You will know the nervous novice phase has passed when someone asks you when to water and you reply, "Well, it depends on the growing conditions . . ."

Fertilizing and feeding

Because succulents grow slowly, most of them don't need additional fertilizer if their soil mixture is well balanced. The exceptions are the tree-dwelling jungle succulents — the epiphyllums, rhipsalis, or schlumbergera (zygocactus). These thrive on a diet of half-strength liquid fertilizer applied as a foliage spray very early in the day. This can be repeated every two weeks during their active growing period. Never apply fertilizer when a plant is dormant or resting.

When a plant is ready for repotting — when the roots have filled the pot and the soil is depleted — it's a good time for very light feeding. Actually, new soil is the best way to fertilze most succulent plants, but since some experts we know also feed their plants at repotting time, we'll pass on their methods. Some simply water the plant thoroughly a week or two after repotting and then apply a liquid fertilizer at half strength. One experienced grower adds bone meal to the soil mix at the rate of one teaspoonful to each six-inch pot. Because it breaks down over a very long time and releases its nutrients to the plant very slowly, he considers it the only safe fertilizer for cacti. Stronger feeding can promote weak, soft growth that is vulnerable to pests and diseases — slow, sturdy growth is healthier.

In landscape plantings, our consultant uses about four pounds of bone meal for every 100 square feet of soil. He digs it into the soil at the time of planting.

Another successful grower soaks a pound of cottonseed meal in five gallons of water for a period of twenty-four hours, then skims off the clear liquid at the top and pours it at the base of those container plants that are not to be repotted at that time. This is a regular spring ritual, along with any necessary repotting chores. He also uses the liquid as a foliar spray for his schlumbergeras (zygocacti).

Whatever the experts use to feed their plants, they all observe these five rules religiously:

1. Never feed a plant during dormancy.

2. Never feed a sick plant.

3. Never feed a plant that is not rooted.

4. Never feed a plant that has just been repotted. (Incorporating bone meal into the soil mix is the one exception.)

5. Always water a plant before fertilizing, even when applying a liquid fertilizer.

Landscape plantings to which no new soil is added can be fed with a commercial liquid fertilizer diluted to half the strength recommended on the label. If leaf mold is available, mix in a little bone meal with the leaf mold on a one to thirty ratio and use it as a mulch.

Pests and disease

Preventing problems is nearly always easier and less time-consuming than trying to cure them. The first rule for preventing plant pests and diseases from establishing themselves in your collection is *cleanliness*. Basic cleanliness eliminates the places that pests might establish themselves before settling down to feasting on your plants.

The second rule is *space*. Space permits good air circulation, but the avid collector often finds this rule difficult to follow. As your interest grows, your collection also grows. There gets to be less and less space for potted specimens and less and less time for maintenance. Resist the temptation to acquire more plants than you can maintain in a clean, healthy environment. If your character is strong, your problems with pests and diseases will be few. But if you're like the rest of us, or your collection is already big enough to render that bit of advice useless, read on.

The best way to guarantee that pests don't get a foothold in your collection is to make the application of a systemic a part of your regular maintenance program. Systemics are pesticides that are absorbed into the plant tissues and kill any pests that try to eat the plant. Systemics can be applied as drenches or as granules followed by watering into the soil. Some sprays also have a slight systemic or residual action.

If the pests become established before your systemic program did, here's how to deal with them, pest by pest.

Ants themselves do not damage plants, but they have an unattractive custom of importing creatures — aphids and scale — that do cause serious damage. Ants transport aphids and scale to convenient plants where the pests colonize. The ants then return to collect a secretion called "honeydew" from their herds. If you eliminate ants from your collection you will probably eliminate a lot of potential problems. Household ant sprays are fine on the surfaces around your plants but not on the plants themselves.

Aphids usually appear on new growth and on flower stalks, buds, and blossoms in the spring. Echeverias and kalanchoes are particularly vulnerable. Aphids are easy to eliminate. A spray of soapy water will do the job if there are not too many; if the infestation is heavy, use a houseplant insect spray and follow label directions. Some succulent species are very sensitive to chemical sprays; be particularly careful with crassulas, echeverias, or kalanchoes when spraying.

Mealy bugs are found on the undersides of leaves, in leaf or stem axils, or the areoles on cacti. They are sucking insects with a waxy protective coating and any insecticide used to kill them must penetrate that coating. Use a household insect spray registered for use on succulents. Follow label directions.

Red spider mites are so tiny that they are for all practical purposes invisible; you recognize their presence from the disfiguring effect they have on your plants. There are two ways to verify your diagnosis. One is to look carefully for the other two succulent pests, mealy bugs and aphids, both of which are visible. If you can't find any, check the undersides of the foliage with a magnifying glass to see if the tiny spider mites are present. Another diagnostic method is to place a sheet of white paper under the plant and shake it gently; some of the spider mites will fall off the plant onto the white paper where they will be much easier to see. To get rid of them, use a registered product containing Kelthane, another miticide.

Slugs and snails are normally only a problem on outdoor plants and in certain areas of the country. Snails and slugs cause mechanical-looking damage — holes in the leaves, or evidence as if the plant had been scraped with a blunt fingernail. Use any good snail bait, and place it on a lettuce leaf near your plants. Don't put bait in your pots; it will attract snails and slugs, and there's the awful possibility that they'll prefer your plant to the bait. The lettuce leaf has the added advantage of being easy to pick up and discard along with the vanquished snails.

Rot is the one disease to which succulents are commonly susceptible. If it has spread through the plant, you will have to cut off the unaffected, healthy part and reroot. Dust the cut surface with a fungicide registered for this use and proceed as you would normally for stem or leaf propagation. You can also graft the healthy section to a vigorous understock.
(See page 92.)

If the root system has begun to rot, cut off the infected roots, dust the remaining roots with a fungicide registered with this use, and repot in a fresh, sterilized potting mix. (See page 86 for repotting instructions.) Don't water the plant for several days.

The worst damage that occurs to succulents is usually mechanical. Succulents bruise easily, and though the wound may heal, it always leaves a scar. Sometimes the scarred or broken leaf can be removed without seriously affecting the plant's appearance, for example, a broken leaf on a sedum or a crassula. On other plants, such as a barrel cactus or an *Agave victoriae-reginae,* there's nothing to do but tell yourself it adds character, and vow to put your remaining perfect specimens in a protected place.

It's easier for the beginner to accept the sense of uncertainty he may have about growing techniques if, along with his succulents, he cultivates the attitude that there is nothing he can't do, just some things he hasn't done yet. If there is a single general rule to follow with succulents, it's "Don't fuss — enjoy."

Propagation

Succulent plants are among the easiest of all plants to propagate. This section is designed to give you the basic techniques of propagation of cuttings, offsets, and from seed. Propagating succulents is fun whether you do it for gifts for friends, to swap with other collectors for plants you don't have, or just to watch them grow. One of the reasons it's fun is because it's easy; succulents are a tough and determined lot, and broken off pieces will root themselves even under the most unlikely circumstances.

The fastest and easiest way to multiply plants is by division. Many succulents, such as echeverias, produce offsets (small plants that cluster around the mother plant). These can be removed and rooted very simply. Stem cuttings, leaf cuttings (pieces of leaves), or leaf starts (whole leaves) all root and produce small plantlets with no elaborate equipment, no expensive supplies, and remarkably little attention. Some succulents, such as the mamillarias and kalanchoes, are so prolific that you might run out of friends, neighbors, and relatives who are willing to become adoptive parents. A few succulents that do not produce offsets and don't propagate readily from cuttings can be propagated by grafting.

Rooting offsets is probably the simplest way to increase your collection. Mamillarias, rebutias, and echinopsis make numerous offsets. The popular peanut cactus *(Chamaecereus sylvestri)* forms many "babies" that separate easily from the parent and, once rooted, develop quickly into mature plants.

Begin by removing the offset from the parent plant by twisting it gently off the stem. Allow it to dry a few days to callus the wound — exactly how long depends on the size and thickness of the plant. It will form a thin, pale brown skin. To prevent rot, dust the exposed area with a fungicide. Dry the offset on a wire rack out of the sun, someplace where the air circulation is good. Quarter-inch mesh hardware cloth makes a satisfactory rack surface.

When the callus is formed, plant the offset in whichever potting formula is suitable to the species; #2 will do for most (see page 86). Prepare your rooting soil in advance and moisten it slightly so that it is damp and crumbly — not sodden. Keep the soil just barely damp and provide good air circulation and morning misting.

If you do not have a greenhouse or space is limited, a simple box frame can be constructed out of a dozen pieces of redwood lath. Cover the frame (the top and all four sides) with clear sheet plastic. Even plastic wrap will do in a pinch. Punch a few holes in the top and sides for ventilation, and voilà — a mini-greenhouse. Place this over the new starts in the morning and remove it in the afternoon to give the foliage time to dry out before temperatures drop in the evening. Keep

An indoor light unit will hold many small specimens, and is great for collectors with limited space. Seedlings also respond well to indoor light culture.

your rooting project out of direct sun, especially with the mini-greenhouse.

After two or three weeks, you can reduce the amount of time the offsets spend in the "nursery" and increase the amount of moisture in the soil. By the end of four of five weeks they can be left uncovered completely. A constant temperature of 70°-75°F (22-24°C) is ideal for quick rooting. To find out if they've begun to root, give each plantlet a *very gentle* tug — slight resistence means it's rooting. Once they've rooted, make the transition into brighter light by degrees over a period of a week. Check the cultural chart for the correct amount of light to give the species you're propagating.

Stem cuttings are the easiest way to propagate plants that don't produce offsets. You will need a very sharp blade — a pruning knife, a razor, or pruning shears — and a sterilizing solution such as diluted bleach or rubbing alcohol. Take, if possible, a narrow stem. The younger shoots on a shrubby succulent or the smaller, thinner stems (the body) of a cactus are best. The smaller the surface of the cut, the less time it takes to callus. Dust the cut surface lightly with rooting hormone or fungicide to prevent rot. It's handy to keep around a small, soft, nylon paint brush to apply whatever preparation you use. Follow the same procedure for drying (callusing) and rooting as outlined for offsets. Most thick-stemmed cacti and euphorbias require about two weeks to callus. The thin-stemmed types and the jungle species need only five to ten days, depending on the weather. All types callus faster in warm, dry weather and take longer in cool, damp weather.

Be sure not to let them dry out too much. Left too long, the thin-stemmed species, such as the epiphytic cacti, could dry out entirely. The main purpose is to expose the cut to warm, dry, circulating air.

Most species will root well in #2 potting soil (regular formula) — the jungle species (the epiphytic cacti) will do best in #3 potting mix (extra-rich).

If you find yourself working with a species that is more prone to rot than root, several experts recommend using horticultural pumice. Burt Greenburg, an expert on rare plants and cycads, uses it for rooting plants collected in the wild which often have difficulty adjusting to domestication. Eleanor Barker of the Cactus and Succulent Society of Palos Verdes uses pumice for rare and valuable species that are difficult to propagate.

If you have difficulty finding pumice, check with specialist nurseries or try writing to the distributor listed on page 23.

Leaf cuttings are as easy to propagate as stem cuttings for many species, like the gasterias and sansevierias. Make clean cuts and follow the same drying procedures used for offsets and stem cuttings.

Be careful when drying leaf cuttings to note which end is up —it's usually easy to identify the right side to root of the top of the leaf or the base of the leaf but it can get tricky with the middle section. Pieces won't root if inserted in the rooting medium upside down. One easy way is to mark your drying rack "top" and "bottom" with masking tape and then arrange the leaf sections exactly as they were cut.

It generally takes no more than two to five days for leaf sections to callus, depending on the size and succulence of the plant — the thick, juicy ones usually take longest. Once callused, they should be pressed firmly into the appropriate rooting medium for that species. Follow the same procedure as with offsets and stem cuttings. The cuttings will form roots — how long it takes depends on the species — and after the leaf section is rooted, a new plantlet will appear at the base of the cutting.

Leaf starts. Leaves of aeonium, sempervivum, adromischus, and many other of the rosette types will not propagate by leaf sections but will reproduce from whole leaves removed from the base of the parent plant. Look for the biggest, fattest leaf you can find and gently twist it off. Allow it to dry two or three days on a wire rack before putting it in the rooting medium. Insert the lower one third of the leaf in the soil mixture — the leaf will root and a new shoot will appear. One word of caution: different species take different amounts of time to root and produce a new plantlet. Some like *Sedum morganianum*, the burro's-tail, root easily and quickly just by tucking the jelly-bean-like leaves into the soil, barely covering them at the base. Others, such as *Hoya carnosa*, take much, much longer. Hoyas root so much more readily from stem cuttings, that it seems a waste of time to try to propagate them from leaf cuttings.

Cuttings and offsets can be started in community containers — that is, several cuttings of the same plant in one pot or flat. Or, they can be started individually in small plastic pots. Plastic pots are preferable to clay ones because they help keep the soil evenly moist longer.

Plants started by any of the above methods — offsets, stem cuttings, leaf cuttings, and leaf starts — all produce plants identical to the parent plant. If you have a specimen with some especially attractive characteristic, asexual vegetative reproduction is the only certain way of propagating the plant and retaining that characteristic. Seeds, in accordance with the laws of genetics, take characteristics from both parent plants, and resulting seedlings are rarely identical to either.

Propagation from seed is not difficult for most species of cacti and other succulents. You generally get many more plants but the time from germination to maturity can be three to seven years. The stages in between are absorbing, though, and if you have grown anything from seed before, you know it's half the fun of growing plants. Forget about how long it will be until you have a flowering specimen — there's a vast amount to be seen from the first thrust of life to a sturdy young plant.

Start with fresh viable seed. If the seed is old, it won't be your fault if you get zero germination but it is unnecessarily discouraging.

Your supplies and tools should all be sterilized, and the potting mix you use should be free of pests, diseases, and weed seeds.

A good way to start seeds is to use a plastic sandwich box or refrigerator "left over" storage box with a fitted lid. Punch lots of holes in the bottom for drainage, including one at each corner. Put in a layer of sponge rock or activated charcoal or coarse granite and fine-grade drainage material. On top of this drainage layer pour a very lean, gritty soil mix. Two parts coarse sand and ½ part pulverized leaf mold or peat will do the job. This is rich enough to get seeds of any species started, and if you're dealing with plants that ordinarily require a richer medium, the seedlings can be pricked out of this mixture and potted up in richer soil when they have a bit of growth on them.

Before you put the seeds on the seed bed, press it lightly to make it firm and make sure that it is smooth and even across the top. Sprinkle the seeds over the surface of the soil. If the seeds are very tiny, using a fold of paper to hold them while you sprinkle will be easier than using your hands. Some experts scatter a very thin covering of sand over the seeds; some prefer not to. Try it both ways to see which works best for you.

Moisten the soil by placing the container in a shallow pan of luke-

Starting succulents from seed may be too time-consuming for some gardeners, but it's a worthwhile experience and results in large quantity of seedlings.

To graft: Start with clean tools and botanically compatible plants.

Cut scion off. Make sure it's smaller than the understock.

Carefully cut the top of the understock off; protect fingers with padding.

Attach scion, cut side down, to understock. Make sure union meets evenly.

Hold scion in place with a rubber band around pot and plant, but not too tightly.

The understock and the scion "donor" stand behind the new grafted plant.

warm or room-temperature water. The soil will absorb the water through the drain holes in the bottom. When the soil begins to look moist on the surface, remove the box from the water, and put the lid on the box. For the best and fastest germination, provide a constant bottom heat of 70°F.

Under natural conditions, seeds germinate in damp, sheltered places, usually at the base of a larger plant that provides sufficient shade to keep the soil moist enough to maintain the tiny seedlings after germination. Even the dryest-growing species must have moisture available during the seedling stage. At the same time, seedlings are vulnerable to a disease called damping-off, a fungus that attacks the new plant at the base.

To maintain the delicate balance between too much moisture and too little it's essential to provide good air circulation by removing the lid of the germinating box as soon as germination has taken place. The air circulation helps the moisture to evaporate from the soil surface and helps keep excess moisture from building up.

Grafting

Grafting is a procedure that unites two different plants into a single plant. There are two reasons for grafting: emergency grafting to save the life of the plant and elective grafting to change the appearance of the plant.

Emergency grafting is done to save a plant with a rotted root system or lower stem. It might also be necessary for rooting collected plants which do not root successfully out of their native habitat. Grafting is valuable as a means of propagating a valuable plant that does not produce offsets and takes many years to mature, bloom, and set seed.

Elective or cosmetic grafting is used to change the form of the plant or to speed up propagation of stem cuttings.

The process itself consists of uniting a *scion* (stem cutting) and an *understock* (the root system) of two different plants. The understock gives vigor and strength to the weak or slow-rooting scion. The two plants must be botanically compatible, (from the same botanical family) even though they are often of different species within a family. You cannot graft a cactus to a crassula but you can graft one kind of cactus to another kind of cactus. Plants should be grafted during their period of growth and never when the understock is dormant.

The success of the graft depends on three factors: absolute cleanliness, a close fit between the growth layers of scion and understock, and maintaining the close union of the two pieces until they have grown together. It's essential to have the scion and understock closely matched in size in order to have as much of the cut surface of both in contact and to work as quickly as possible to prevent both callusing and exposure to disease. Have everything you need assembled and sterilized before you make any cuts. Use sharp tools that will make a clean, straight cut.

There are four different types of graft cuts. Which you use is determined by the size and shape of the plants you're grafting.

The flat cut is used for thick, globular scions and is the easiest to do. It is important for the understock to be large enough to support the scion both at the time of grafting and as both plants mature. As a general rule, the stock should be a minimum of ten times the weight of the scion. The scion can be smaller in diameter than the understock but never larger. Rubber bands are the easiest way to hold flat grafts. Pass the band over the scion and under the pot on two sides.

Another technique is to insert a strong, pointed spine on both sides of the understock. Then pass the rubber band over the scion and attach it to the spines on either side of the understock. Toothpicks can also be used but spines have the advantage of disappearing without leaving a mark, while toothpicks leave a scar. Be sure that the bands are not too tight or the scion will be injured.

Because they are flexible, rubber bands can expand with the growth of the scion though they typically rot away after growth begins.

The cleft cut is used to give a draping variety an upright growth habit. Specialist nurseryman Rogers Weld of Fernwood Gardens in Southern California uses a hybrid opuntia, 'Mrs. Burbank,' as the understock for a schlumbergera scion.

The side cut is used for upright, cylindrical plants, and is almost as easy as the flat graft.

The stab graft is used to unite a schlumbergera to an opuntia pad by making a cut at the areole of the opuntia and inserting the schlumbergera. It is the least common type of graft.

Until a graft has taken, avoid overhead watering; water in the cut is an open invitation to rot.

Step-by-step

Grafting procedures

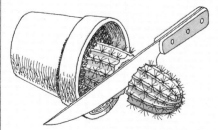

A. Cut the top off of stock plant.

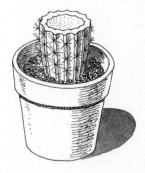

B. Trim the stock cut to assure a flat, clean surface.

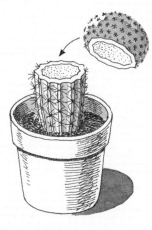

C. Place the scion cut on the stock. Make sure the thin ring of conductive tissue is matched up, or at least overlapping or touching on all parts.

D. Secure new graft with rubber band to assure good scion-to-stock contact and a successful graft.

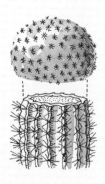

FLAT GRAFT

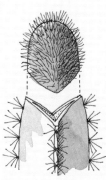

CLEFT GRAFT

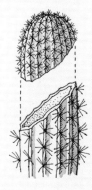

SIDE GRAFT

Guide to growing cactus and succulents

NAME OF PLANT AND TEMPERATURE RANGE	SOIL MIX			LIGHT REQUIREMENT				HUMIDITY TOLERANCE				WATER REQUIREMENTS			EASE OF CULTURE			MOST ATTRACTIVE FEATURE		
	Gritty/lean	Gritty/rich	Rich	Direct sun	Winter direct sun	Bright	Moderate	Very dry	Average	Moist	Very moist	Dry out between waterings	Approach dryness between waterings	Keep evenly moist	Easy to grow	Moderately difficult	Very difficult	Form	Foliage	Flower
Abromeitiella (High °F: 95 — Low °F: 25)																				
Acanthocalycium (High °F: 100 — Low °F: 25)																				
Adenia (High °F: 90 — Low °F: 40)																				
Adromischus (High °F: 90 — Low °F: 40)																				
Aeonium (High °F: 80 — Low °F: 35)																				
Agave (High °F: 90 — Low °F: 30)																				
Aloe (High °F: 90 — Low °F: 35)																				
Anacampseros (High °F: 90 — Low °F: 35)																				
Aporocactus (High °F: 90 — Low °F: 35)																				
Ariocarpus (High °F: 100 — Low °F: 30)																				
Astrophytum (High °F: 90 — Low °F: 30)																				
Aztekium (High °F: 90 — Low °F: 35)																				
Beaucarnea (High °F: 90 — Low °F: 35)																				
Bowiea (High °F: 90 — Low °F: 35)																				
Bolivicereus (High °F: 90 — Low °F: 35)																				
Bursera (High °F: 100 — Low °F: 25)																				
Caralluma (High °F: 90 — Low °F: 35)																				
Cephalocereus (High °F: 100 — Low °F: 35)																				
Cereus (High °F: 90 — Low °F: 25)																				
Ceropegia (High °F: 90 — Low °F: 35)																				
Chamaecereus (High °F: 90 — Low °F: 25)																				
Cleistocactus (High °F: 100 — Low °F: 35)																				
Cochemiea (High °F: 100 — Low °F: 35)																				
Conophytum (High °F: 90 — Low °F: 35)																				
Copiapoa (High °F: 100 — Low °F: 20)																				
Coryphantha (High °F: 90 — Low °F: 35)																				
Cotyledon (High °F: 90 — Low °F: 35)																				
Crassula (High °F: 90 — Low °F: 35)																				
Cynanchum (High °F: 90 — Low °F: 40)																				
Dasylirion (High °F: 90 — Low °F: 35)																				
Dintheranthus (High °F: 85 — Low °F: 35)																				
Dioscorea (High °F: 95 — Low °F: 25)																				
Diploycyatha (High °F: 95 — Low °F: 25)																				
Dudleya (High °F: 90 — Low °F: 25)																				
Echeveria (High °F: 85 — Low °F: 25)																				
Echinocactus (High °F: 95 — Low °F: 20)																				
Echinocereus (High °F: 95 — Low °F: 20)																				
Echinopsis (High °F: 90 — Low °F: 25)																				
Edithcolea (High °F: 85 — Low °F: 45)																				
Epithelantha (High °F: 90 — Low °F: 25)																				
Escobaria (High °F: 90 — Low °F: 20)																				
Espostoa (High °F: 85 — Low °F: 35)																				
Euphorbia (High °F: 90 — Low °F: 35)																				
Fenestraria (High °F: 85 — Low °F: 35)																				
Faucaria (High °F: 85 — Low °F: 35)																				
Fouquieria (High °F: 85 — Low °F: 40)																				
Ferocactus (High °F: 90 — Low °F: 35)																				
Frailea (High °F: 90 — Low °F: 35)																				

NAME OF PLANT AND TEMPERATURE RANGE	SOIL MIX			LIGHT REQUIREMENT				HUMIDITY TOLERANCE				WATER REQUIREMENTS			EASE OF CULTURE			MOST ATTRACTIVE FEATURE		
	Gritty/lean	Gritty/rich	Rich	Direct sun	Winter direct sun	Bright	Moderate	Very dry	Average	Moist	Very moist	Dry out between waterings	Approach dryness between waterings	Keep evenly moist	Easy to grow	Moderately difficult	Very difficult	Form	Foliage	Flower
Gasteria (High °F: 90 — Low °F: 30)			X				X		X				X		X				X	
Graptopetalum (High °F: 85 — Low °F: 35)						X			X				X		X			X		
Gymnocalycium (High °F: 85 — Low °F: 30)		X				X			X				X		X			X		
Hamatocactus (High °F: 90 — Low °F: 35)	X			X				X				X			X					X
Hatiora (High °F: 85 — Low °F: 35)			X				X			X				X	X					X
Haworthia (High °F: 85 — Low °F: 35)		X				X			X				X		X				X	
Homalocephala (High °F: 95 — Low °F: 30)	X			X				X				X			X			X		
Huernia (High °F: 85 — Low °F: 35)		X				X			X				X		X					X
Hylocereus (High °F: 85 — Low °F: 35)			X				X			X				X	X					X
Jatropha (High °F: 90 — Low °F: 35)			X			X			X				X			X		X		
Kalanchoe (High °F: 85 — Low °F: 40)		X				X			X				X		X				X	
Kleina (High °F: 90 — Low °F: 35)	X					X		X				X			X				X	
Lapidaria (High °F: 90 — Low °F: 35)	X				X			X				X				X		X		
Lemaireocereus (High °F: 90 — Low °F: 35)	X			X				X				X			X			X		
Leuchtenbergia (High °F: 90 — Low °F: 30)	X				X			X					X			X		X		
Lithops (High °F: 85 — Low °F: 30)	X				X			X				X			X			X		
Lobivia (High °F: 85 — Low °F: 25)		X				X			X				X		X					X
Lophocereus (High °F: 90 — Low °F: 35)	X			X				X				X			X			X		
Mammillaria (High °F: 90 — Low °F: 30)		X				X			X				X		X					X
Mammilopsis (High °F: 85 — Low °F: 20)		X				X			X				X			X				X
Melocactus (High °F: 85 — Low °F: 50)		X		X				X				X				X		X		
Myrtillocactus (High °F: 90 — Low °F: 35)	X			X				X				X			X			X		
Neobesseya (High °F: 85 — Low °F: 20)		X				X			X				X		X					X
Neochilena (High °F: 90 — Low °F: 25)	X					X			X				X		X					X
Neoporteria (High °F: 90 — Low °F: 25)	X					X			X				X		X					X
Notocactus (High °F: 90 — Low °F: 30)		X				X			X				X		X					X
Nyctocereus (High °F: 90 — Low °F: 35)		X				X			X				X		X					X
Opuntia (High °F: 90 — Low °F: 30)	X			X				X				X			X			X		
Oreocereus (High °F: 85 — Low °F: 25)	X			X				X				X			X			X		
Pachycereus (High °F: 90 — Low °F: 35)	X			X				X				X			X			X		
Pachyphytum (High °F: 85 — Low °F: 35)		X				X			X				X		X				X	
Pachypodium (High °F: 90 — Low °F: 50)		X				X			X				X			X		X		
Pachyveria (High °F: 85 — Low °F: 35)		X				X			X				X		X				X	
Parodia (High °F: 85 — Low °F: 25)		X				X			X				X		X					X
Pelargonium (High °F: 90 — Low °F: 30)			X			X			X				X		X					X
Pelecyphora (High °F: 90 — Low °F: 35)	X				X			X				X				X		X		
Pleiospilos (High °F: 90 — Low °F: 35)	X				X			X				X				X		X		
Portulacaria (High °F: 90 — Low °F: 35)		X				X			X				X		X				X	
Rebutia (High °F: 85 — Low °F: 25)		X				X			X				X		X					X
Rhombophyllum (High °F: 90 — Low °F: 35)	X				X			X				X				X		X		
Scilla (High °F: 85 — Low °F: 35)			X			X			X				X		X				X	
Sedum (High °F: 85 — Low °F: 35)		X				X			X				X		X				X	
Selinicereus (High °F: 85 — Low °F: 35)			X			X				X				X	X					X
Sempervivum (High °F: 80 — Low °F: 30)		X				X			X				X		X				X	
Senecio (High °F: 85 — Low °F: 35)			X			X			X				X		X				X	
Setiechinopsis (High °F: 90 — Low °F: 30)		X				X			X				X		X					X
Stapelia (High °F: 105 — Low °F: 35)		X				X			X				X			X				X
Thelocactus (High °F: 120 — Low °F: 25)	X			X				X				X			X					X
Trichocereus (High °F: 120 — Low °F: 25)		X		X				X				X			X					X
Trichodiadema (High °F: 120 — Low °F: 30)		X				X			X				X		X				X	
Turbinicarpus (High °F: 120 — Low °F: 28)	X					X		X				X			X					X

Common name index